From Pushchair to Ploughshare: a Yorkshire Farmer's Tale

John D Taylor

JOHN D TAYLOR

First published in 2014 by Clio Publishing, Dorset, England.

http://www.cliopublishing.org

A full CIP record for this book is available from the British Library.

ISBN: 978-1-78280-284-6

Designed and typeset by CARBON DESiGN company // www.carbon.uk.com
Printed by Hobbs the Printer Ltd, Southampton, England.
www.hobbscolour.co.uk

Clio Publishing is committed to a sustainable future for our business, readers
and the planet. The book in your hands is made from paper certified by the
Forest Stewardship Council.

To the memory of my son,
Jonathan David Taylor, 1976-1988

About the Author

John Taylor was born on the 5th July 1937 and from the ages of two to six-and-a-half spent the Second World War living in a rented farmhouse in Nidderdale, Yorkshire. Life in the countryside instilled in him a love of farming which later became an ambition to be a farmer. Though six years older, his brother also had the same wish, and with parents who wanted the best for their sons, they joined forces and bought a farm in 1952.

Working very long hours the two brothers gradually built up a farm, which though very small by today's standards, continued to thrive until size began to matter and other means were required to increase their income. John had become interested in computers and developed England's first operational online livestock auction, several years before the internet became available for such a venture.

The tragic death of his 12-year-old son and subsequent divorce forced the sale of the farm and led him to seek yet more sources of income, many of which are detailed in this book. Retirement and his re-marriage opened up new interests, which in turn revealed undiscovered abilities, one of which was writing his memoir. Only the reader can judge whether it is in fact an ability or a liability.

Contents

Part Three

Acknowledgements

There are many people who have helped me throughout my life and continue to be important to me.

First and foremost is my mother Irene, and father Sydney, who were prepared to sell their home to enable us to buy the farm. I cannot adequately express the thanks I owe to my brother Geoff, who has always been there for me when I needed him; no matter where he was or what he was doing, he found time for me. My cousin Mike, who despite all the scrapes I got him into over the years has always been a genuine and loyal pal, in fact we are more like brothers than cousins.

There were also people such as the manager of Barkers & Lee Smith whom in 1952, had enough faith in us to sell seed corn and cattle feed to us on deferred payment terms, interest free for a year or until we sold the resulting crop. Syd Bays, who as a complete surprise bought and had delivered to us five in-pig Gilts, telling us we needn't pay for them until we sold their litters. Peter Kirkwood, one of the most progressive farmers I know, who entered 80 of his pigs as the first lot to be sold on Tabrotec and who loyally continued to support the Auction with entries every week until it closed down.

More recently deserving my special thanks for her professional guidance and friendly advice is my publisher, Dr Susan England of Clio Publishing; without her help this book would never have seen the light of day nor had print put on to paper. Also my friend Sam Walton who I supplied with word processors and computers for many years; it was Sam who put me in touch with Susan so encouraging me to finish the book. John Somers of Carbon Design company who by his expertise turned my story into a book.

My genuine thanks go to my first wife Angela, who gave me three wonderful children and helped to bring them up and made me the proudest father in the world. Also Angela's mother, Dorothy who helped to finance her grandchildren's education from which their hard work took them on to university and into their chosen careers.

Most importantly, I say thank you to Irene, who has awakened in me a love of the arts and classics of literature and music, together with a realisation that I could actually do some of the things which I had always thought were beyond me. She continues to give me love, support and encouragement, showing me there was light at the end of my personal tunnel; without her it would have been a cave and I would now be a hermit. If it had not been for our mutual friend Jenny Billany's wish to tidy up the lives of two of her friends we would never have met. She and husband Mike together with very our good friends Ray and Julie Newmarch, Pat (Patricia) Lawson and Mike and Carol Bartlett, all who constitute the self-styled 'Sideliners', continue to provide life with many truly joyful and memorable experiences. I also have very happy memories of family friends, Norma and Alan Morton, and Pat and Rosemarie Bailey, particularly the dinner parties we held at each other's houses when the children were growing up.

My greatest personal thanks must go to my daughters, Sally and Helen, their husbands Adam and Alan, and my grandchildren, Jessica, Emily, Keira and Harry. I owe you all a lifetime of gratitude for making me so proud to be called your Dad, proper Grandad or just plain Grandad. This book is primarily written for you with all my love.

Foreword

I am delighted to write the Foreword for John Taylor's book as I have known him for more years than either of us would care to remember. In that time I have regarded him as a friend, an entrepreneur, a farmer of note, a raconteur, a historian and an intrepid traveller. Aside from his farming background, he attended Hull Building College where he learned the skills that would later enable him to build his own house. John has, along with his brother, Geoff, farmed cows, chickens and pigs, and set up the very first operational computerised auction service in England. I saw it in operation at several livestock markets and it was way ahead of its time. Establishing Tabrotec, (Taylor Bros Technology) was the first introduction for many farmers and others to computer technology. In fact I bought my first word processor from John, before venturing on to computers. He was an excellent mentor and if there was a problem, he could put his finger on it immediately. Having tragically lost his 12-year-old son in a farm accident, and subsequent divorce three years later, he sold the farm, and the closure of Tabrotec followed not too long after. Since then, John with Irene, his second wife have travelled to a host of countries that include Canada, USA, Russia, and New Zealand. He gives excellent presentations on these travels and I know his book will be a delight.

Sam Walton, May 2014.

Mike and Geoff

This story records the family history up to the 1930s and brought up to date by the author's own experiences of a childhood spent on a 300-year old farm in the Yorkshire Dales. Without any mains services the farm was operated by men and horses – no tractors.

Moving back to East Yorkshire where agriculture was being mechanised the seeds were sown for an interest in farming which became an occupation. This industry is dependent on market forces as this book clearly shows. The unpredictable nature of farming affects the lives of all those involved who have to be able to adapt to different circumstances and modern technology. Embracing these changes has led to new enterprises and a complete life change.

Reading the story of John's life you can only admire his tenacity and cheerfulness.

Mike Bartlett, May 2014

Reading this book has brought back many memories; some events I thought I had forgotten, and some which take on a new perspective with the distance of time. It is interesting to note which ones each of us have individually found memorable.

From a very young age, John and I both knew we wanted to be farmers. After we left our wartime home in Nidderdale our lives took different routes – John worked on farms in the locality of Ganstead, where he lived, and I studied for a year at Askham Bryan Agricultural College followed by six years on farms in the Driffield area. Then in 1956 we joined forces in the purchase of Hill Farm at Thirtleby.

We worked together for the next 30 years, sharing each other's company for up to 12 hours a day, six or seven days a week, and I am proud to say that in all that time we never exchanged a cross word. Whether new ideas came up or we encountered problems, we always talked things through amicably until we agreed on the way forward. That is still true to this day.

For all our lives we have been lucky to have cousin Mike by our side, either living next door or working with Taylor Brothers. Because they are so close in age, Mike has been virtually another brother for John.

Since our retirement, our lives have diverged again but we still look forward to meeting up twice a month for Probus in Hedon. As the book shows, there have been some black days for us to look back on, but there are many more bright and happy ones. I hope you will enjoy reading about all of them.

Geoff Taylor, May 2014.

The Three Old Boys 'scrubbed up'.
Left to right, Mike, Geoff, and the author John.

My Family Tree 1752-2014

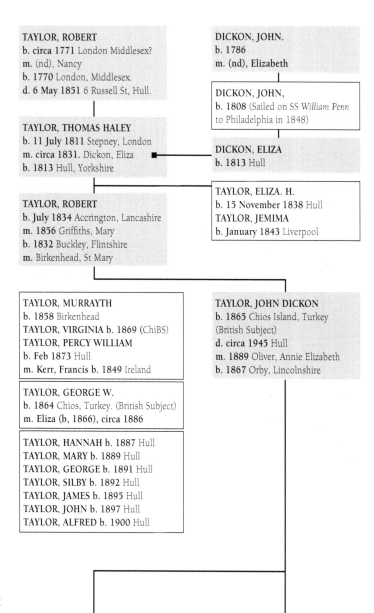

TAYLOR, ROBERT
b. circa 1771 London Middlesex?
m. (nd), Nancy
b. 1770 London, Middlesex.
d. 6 May 1851 6 Russell St, Hull.

TAYLOR, THOMAS HALEY
b. 11 July 1811 Stepney, London
m. circa 1831. Dickon, Eliza
b. 1813 Hull, Yorkshire

TAYLOR, ROBERT
b. July 1834 Accrington, Lancashire
m. 1856 Griffiths, Mary
b. 1832 Buckley, Flintshire
m. Birkenhead, St Mary

DICKON, JOHN.
b. 1786
m. (nd), Elizabeth

DICKON, JOHN,
b. 1808 (Sailed on SS *William Penn* to Philadelphia in 1848)

DICKON, ELIZA
b. 1813 Hull

TAYLOR, ELIZA. H.
b. 15 November 1838 Hull
TAYLOR, JEMIMA
b. January 1843 Liverpool

TAYLOR, MURRAYTH
b. 1858 Birkenhead
TAYLOR, VIRGINIA b. 1869 (ChiBS)
TAYLOR, PERCY WILLIAM
b. Feb 1873 Hull
m. Kerr, Francis b. 1849 Ireland

TAYLOR, GEORGE W.
b. 1864 Chios, Turkey. (British Subject)
m. Eliza (b, 1866), circa 1886

TAYLOR, HANNAH b. 1887 Hull
TAYLOR, MARY b. 1889 Hull
TAYLOR, GEORGE b. 1891 Hull
TAYLOR, SILBY b. 1892 Hull
TAYLOR, JAMES b. 1895 Hull
TAYLOR, JOHN b. 1897 Hull
TAYLOR, ALFRED b. 1900 Hull

TAYLOR, JOHN DICKON
b. 1865 Chios Island, Turkey
(British Subject)
d. circa 1945 Hull
m. 1889 Oliver, Annie Elizabeth
b. 1867 Orby, Lincolnshire

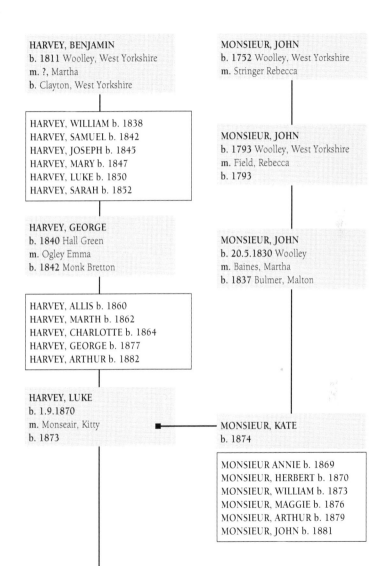

HARVEY, BENJAMIN
b. 1811 Woolley, West Yorkshire
m. ?, Martha
b. Clayton, West Yorkshire

HARVEY, WILLIAM b. 1838
HARVEY, SAMUEL b. 1842
HARVEY, JOSEPH b. 1845
HARVEY, MARY b. 1847
HARVEY, LUKE b. 1850
HARVEY, SARAH b. 1852

HARVEY, GEORGE
b. 1840 Hall Green
m. Ogley Emma
b. 1842 Monk Bretton

HARVEY, ALLIS b. 1860
HARVEY, MARTH b. 1862
HARVEY, CHARLOTTE b. 1864
HARVEY, GEORGE b. 1877
HARVEY, ARTHUR b. 1882

HARVEY, LUKE
b. 1.9.1870
m. Monseair, Kitty
b. 1873

MONSIEUR, JOHN
b. 1752 Woolley, West Yorkshire
m. Stringer Rebecca

MONSIEUR, JOHN
b. 1793 Woolley, West Yorkshire
m. Field, Rebecca
b. 1793

MONSIEUR, JOHN
b. 20.5.1830 Woolley
m. Baines, Martha
b. 1837 Bulmer, Malton

MONSIEUR, KATE
b. 1874

MONSIEUR ANNIE b. 1869
MONSIEUR, HERBERT b. 1870
MONSIEUR, WILLIAM b. 1873
MONSIEUR, MAGGIE b. 1876
MONSIEUR, ARTHUR b. 1879
MONSIEUR, JOHN b. 1881

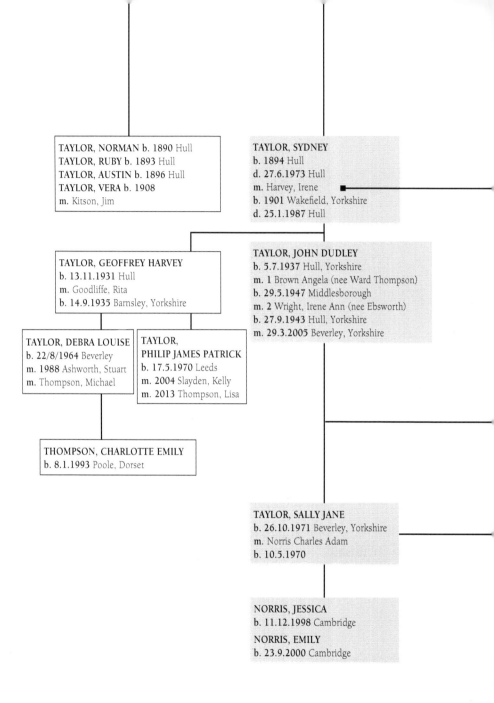

TAYLOR, NORMAN b. 1890 Hull
TAYLOR, RUBY b. 1893 Hull
TAYLOR, AUSTIN b. 1896 Hull
TAYLOR, VERA b. 1908
m. Kitson, Jim

TAYLOR, SYDNEY
b. 1894 Hull
d. 27.6.1973 Hull
m. Harvey, Irene
b. 1901 Wakefield, Yorkshire
d. 25.1.1987 Hull

TAYLOR, GEOFFREY HARVEY
b. 13.11.1931 Hull
m. Goodliffe, Rita
b. 14.9.1935 Barnsley, Yorkshire

TAYLOR, JOHN DUDLEY
b. 5.7.1937 Hull, Yorkshire
m. 1 Brown Angela (nee Ward Thompson)
b. 29.5.1947 Middlesborough
m. 2 Wright, Irene Ann (nee Ebsworth)
b. 27.9.1943 Hull, Yorkshire
m. 29.3.2005 Beverley, Yorkshire

TAYLOR, DEBRA LOUISE
b. 22/8/1964 Beverley
m. 1988 Ashworth, Stuart
m. Thompson, Michael

TAYLOR,
PHILIP JAMES PATRICK
b. 17.5.1970 Leeds
m. 2004 Slayden, Kelly
m. 2013 Thompson, Lisa

THOMPSON, CHARLOTTE EMILY
b. 8.1.1993 Poole, Dorset

TAYLOR, SALLY JANE
b. 26.10.1971 Beverley, Yorkshire
m. Norris Charles Adam
b. 10.5.1970

NORRIS, JESSICA
b. 11.12.1998 Cambridge
NORRIS, EMILY
b. 23.9.2000 Cambridge

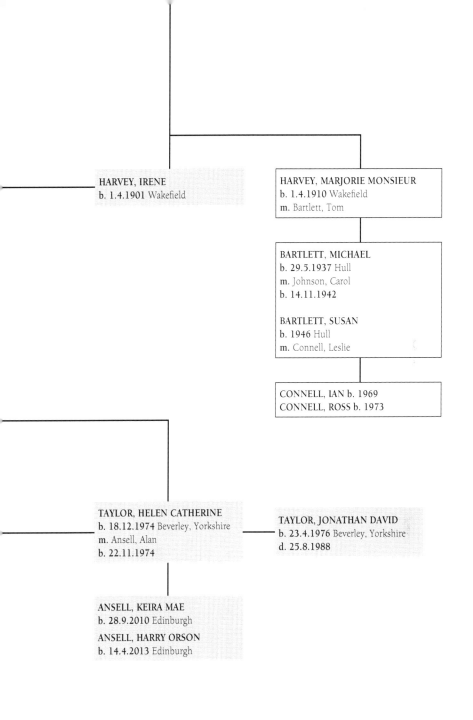

HARVEY, IRENE
b. 1.4.1901 Wakefield

HARVEY, MARJORIE MONSIEUR
b. 1.4.1910 Wakefield
m. Bartlett, Tom

BARTLETT, MICHAEL
b. 29.5.1937 Hull
m. Johnson, Carol
b. 14.11.1942

BARTLETT, SUSAN
b. 1946 Hull
m. Connell, Leslie

CONNELL, IAN b. 1969
CONNELL, ROSS b. 1973

TAYLOR, HELEN CATHERINE
b. 18.12.1974 Beverley, Yorkshire
m. Ansell, Alan
b. 22.11.1974

TAYLOR, JONATHAN DAVID
b. 23.4.1976 Beverley, Yorkshire
d. 25.8.1988

ANSELL, KEIRA MAE
b. 28.9.2010 Edinburgh
ANSELL, HARRY ORSON
b. 14.4.2013 Edinburgh

Family tree notes

Taylor The earliest names are those of Robert Taylor, born in Middlesex, London in 1771, who was to become a master mariner. His wife Nancy lived to the age of 81 and was described as working as an 'Inspector of Houses' when she died on the 8 May 1851 whilst living with her son Thomas and daughter-in-law Eliza neé Dickon at No. 6 Russell Street in Hull.

Dickon Reference to the Dickon family begins with John Dickon, born in 1786. He owned three freehold houses in Grimsby Lane, Hull, and was registered as entitled to vote in the electoral register of 1834. His daughter Eliza married Thomas Taylor in 1831.

Harvey On my Mother's side of the family, Benjamin Harvey was born in 1811 in Woolley, West Yorkshire, and he and his wife Martha had seven children. Their second son George was born in 1840 and was a coal miner and landlord of The Bay Horse Inn at (Tanyard Fold) Hall Green, Crigglestone, West Yorkshire. During his time there he established a boxing club with a ring in the building adjacent to the pub. His eldest son Luke was my grandfather.

Monseair John Monseair born in 1752 (variously spelt Monseer or Monsieur); the family may have originated in the town of Chartres, France, arriving in England during the Huguenot's flight from persecution in France in the 1600s. It was the custom at the time to anglicise their French names when moving to England, for example a name which may have originally been 'Monsieur Jean de Chartre' in France became John Monsieur in England.

Preface

Living alone at the age of 65, I continued to be affected by the death of my twelve year old son in an accident on the family farm, an accident which I believed I should have prevented, leading to the subsequent break-up of what had previously been a very happy marriage.

In an attempt not to dwell on the immediate past I spent time researching my family history, realising that there were a host of stories hidden in the lives of my ancestors. It made me wish I had asked my parents all the questions that I now found intriguing such as, why was Great Grandpa Robert Taylor on the Island of Chios with his wife and family in the 1860s? What was his job? Was it a government post for it must have been important for them to stay there for at least eight years between 1861 and 1869?

With those questions in mind and to lay some of my personal ghosts to rest while at the same time counting my blessings, I decided to write this book recollecting the more amusing incidents and events as well as recording the saddest episodes in my life. Many people will have far more harrowing tales to tell and I hope this book will give them hope for the future and show a way forward that they might like to consider. But I would also hope that descendants of mine will read it and unlike me know what at least one of their ancestors did with his given share of life.

Though I started the process in 2002 I found it impossible to write the chapter about the death of my son Jonathan; my writer's block was only removed when I decided to give a talk on my life to our local Probus Club in 2012. I knew I was going to have to tackle that part of my life story this time and braced myself for the ordeal, and apart from the unavoidable break in my voice as I spoke the words, I used that experience to convince myself I could start to write again.

Part One
1. Formative Nidderdale

Hazel Close was a wonderful place for three small boys to live and play, a place where every tree, every meadow, every rocky outcrop stirred that vivid imagination which makes the years of childhood so precious. In 1939, at the age of two, with my eight year-old brother Geoff, two year-old cousin Mike, together with mothers and maternal grandparents, we begun four-and-a-half truly memorable years living in this beautiful part of Yorkshire.

Seventy-six years later I look back on the sunshine and showers of a life filled with periods of great happiness and times of deep sadness. Incidents often required a sense of humour which was my defence against the wrath of others; I was an early convert to the theory that if you can make people laugh they don't become quite so angry.

At the outbreak of the war our two families lived in adjoining semi-detached bungalows in the village of Ganstead only four miles from the centre of Hull and three miles from the docks, which were a prime target for the German bombers. Dad, who had fought in the First World War, worked for seed merchants in Hull's High Street, at one time sharing his time between two firms, M. M. Hirchfield and Co., and Messrs. Nicholsons. Mike's father, our Uncle Tom, was a fireman in the Hull City fire service, a very difficult and dangerous job especially in wartime.

When nightly reports on the news announced that 'an east coast town' had been hit in an overnight bombing raid they knew immediately which town that was, and consequently were very concerned for our safety. During these raids we were initially advised to take shelter either in the bathroom or under our very stout dining table. Eventually, a concrete and brick air-raid shelter was built in a neighbour's garden, a welcome improvement when following one raid the garden was littered with jagged bomb and shell splinters.

Although they would have to remain at home in Hull for their work, Dad and Uncle Tom were determined that we should move somewhere safer, so an advertisement seeking property to rent was placed in the *Yorkshire Post*, and from approximately 30 replies Auntie Marjorie and my Mother each independently selected Hazel Close. A quick visit by my parents gained their approval and arrangements were made for the move. Wartime restrictions created transport problems so the furniture was taken 80 miles to Middlesmoor on one of Syd Bays, a family friend's lorry, while the four adults and we three children piled into a large taxi. The move from Hull proved very timely, as the docks and the nearby oil refinery were heavily bombed the following night.

Nestling in the hillside below the village of Middlesmoor in upper Nidderdale, only the roof and chimneys of Hazel Close were visible from the narrow road winding up from the market town of Pateley Bridge. The house overlooked hay meadows sloping down to How Stean Gorge, where the waters of How Stean Beck had over thousands of years carved an 80 foot deep rocky canyon on their spectacular way to join the River Nidd.

The excitement of our arrival inevitably led to weeks of exploration, beginning with the house and buildings.

There was no electricity or mains water but oil lamps and water from a spring added to the air of adventure. The large black iron range in the living room provided warmth, ample hot water and cooking facilities, and bath nights now involved the use of a tin bath placed on the multi-coloured

Only the roof and chimney pots were visible from the road,
Hazel Close is in the bottom left of the picture.

rag rug in front of the fire. A wireless powered by two accumulator batteries, which Grandpa alternately each week took up to the village post office to be re-charged, gave us the news and some entertainment. It must have been very worrying for my Mother when we heard those dreaded words, 'a bombing raid last night on an east coast town.'

Down three steps and set into the hillside at the back of the house, was a stone paved pantry with stone shelves and walls; it was always cool even in mid-summer. Off this room another storeroom served as the dairy and the cowshed. As the former was accessible to the farm manager Neil's sheep-dogs, the door between the two was prone to sticking and the tendency was to leave it 'off the hook', much to Grandpa's annoyance as he warned that one day the dogs would get in to the pantry.

On the pantry floor a large earthenware jar was eventually filled with eggs preserved in isinglass,[1] the stone shelves providing ideal cold conditions for the very rare in wartime, but much prized joint of beef, and large hooks in the ceiling for hanging the slightly more frequent salted sides of bacon,

3

ready to be freshly sliced 'straight off the hook and into the pan' for mouth-watering bacon and egg breakfasts truly fit for a king.

The preservation of food stored in the pantry was an essential skill in those days and there always seemed to be supplies sufficient to feed us through a siege, or more likely the probability of being cut off by snowdrifts for several weeks in winter.

Inevitably one day the dairy door was less secure than usual, and this coincided with the arrival of a particularly succulent joint of meat, the unfortunate result being an empty meat plate and two very well-fed sheepdogs. Mum and Aunt Marge's resourcefulness was tested to the full and Grandpa, who never learned the truth, was fooled into thinking that he was eating the joint, when in fact it had been substituted by a cunningly disguised concoction made from tinned corned beef covered with thick gravy. It was one time when the weak light from oil lamps was a boon.

Hazel Close in 1940.

Up narrow wooden stairs, the bedrooms had bare polished wood floors and were furnished by iron bedsteads with shining brass bed knobs, large wardrobes and dressing tables with marble tops completed the furnishings.

4

These had belonged to Grandma and were brought up from home in Hull on the lorry. Thick blankets and feather-filled eiderdowns were essential to keep out the cold. Night time lighting was by candles, and it just didn't do to be afraid of the dark.

A major disadvantage was the location of the toilet, a two-seater model built of white-washed stone, strategically, but unfortunately and especially at night, situated 20 yards from the house, and through the garden gate into the corner of a wood. The wooden door featured a traditional diamond-shaped hole for ventilation and early warning of the approach of other would-be occupants, giving time for a somewhat strained shout of 'I'm in here, I won't be long.' Security was affected simultaneously by use of one's extended foot, not possible until about the age of five when leg length made this attainable without at the same time slipping off the seat.

Alternative night time toilet facilities for us were of the florally decorated porcelain variety, conveniently available adjacent to the bed, although on one very dark night my sleepy use of this facility when I showed a distinct lack of accuracy, caused the flow intended for the receptacle to be directed through a knot hole in the floor falling as a steady stream on to the middle of the green baize covered kitchen table below. It took the adults sitting at the table a few stunned seconds to appreciate the nature of the deluge but no time at all to rush upstairs to identify and apprehend the semi-comatose culprit.

Various outbuildings adjoined the house, the nearest was a cow byre with hayloft above, followed by cart sheds and stables. The cows were hand milked by Neil, who came down from the village every day, providing us with our fresh milk, taking the remainder back up to the road in a churn. In summer this was kept cool by simply being immersed in a stone trough, through which ice cold spring water flowed in a seemingly never-ending stream.

Visits to the byre at milking time were frequently met by a well-aimed jet of warm milk squirted by Neil from the udder of the cow currently being milked. His nickname for me of 'T'owd Fat Man' [2] was an indication of how well-fed we were despite wartime rationing; his cows nutritious unadulterated fresh milk also played a significant part in my obvious wellbeing.

Geoff, 'T'owd Fat Man' (author), and Mike.

Small undulating grass fields between the house and How Stean Gorge, retained their natural contours left by the Ice Age, only slightly softened by hundreds of years of toil by men and horses. These fields provided grazing and sweet-smelling hay, full of natural herbs for the long hard winters. Tractors had not yet entered the scene so the less attractive uniformity of the lowlands had thus far been avoided. One of the fields contained a small fenced area where a spring came to the surface, feeding a pond and a patch of watercress, which became Grandpa's pride and joy. Almost inevitably the day came when Mike and I, knowing how the grown-ups enjoyed their

6

cress, piled our toy wheelbarrows full with the succulent plant, roots and all, and proudly delivered them to the door. Needless to say, hurried re-planting and an early night in bed were the reward for our efforts.

The abundant availability of running water was an irresistible magnet, this coupled with several lengths of rusty iron pipe, which nobody seemed to want, provided us with a less destructive form of play, although to us it was work not play. Thus was born our intricate water diversion scheme; the pipes were butted together end-to-end using mud to make a fairly water tight joint. Mud and small boys tend to be a bit messy but this made it all the more fun, so we spent many happy days on the project, marvelling at our ability to direct water almost anywhere at will. I do not remember getting into trouble over this, so assume we did not flood anywhere too important. In fact Grandpa who had been a well-respected engineer at Reckitt & Coleman's Canister Works in Hull, was I think quite proud of us. At least it kept us away from his beloved watercress beds.

Other less savoury schemes included our 'sawmill', that involved turning my three-wheel bike upside down to expose the rear sprocket and chain. Turning the pedals at speed provided a rudimentary saw that though rather ineffective at cutting wood, could slice through a sun-dried cowpat in no time at all. We soon had a small factory producing the world's finest cow pat slices yet unfortunately we were unable to find a market for our product, even though there was no shortage of the raw material with the cows making fresh deliveries to the fields every day! I am convinced that this and other schemes provided us with an early exposure to a low level of 'natural' infection, providing resistance against many diseases in later life. I was of course, too young to be aware of this theory and so unable to convince my mother of its value at the time.

On week days Geoff, who was then of school age, attended the small village school in Middlesmoor, so summer holidays were the main time family picnics in the hay fields. A particular favourite was to go across about three fields, over stiles and along footpaths lined with dry brittle bracken which crunched under foot, whilst 80 feet below we could hear the roar of water cascading over the rocks of How Stean Gorge. Climbing over stiles in the stone walls we descended through woods filled with bluebells or depending on the time of year, foxgloves and huge buttercups. Our destination was about half-a-mile upstream where the favourite spot to picnic was a grassy bank under the trees, with a large flat rock which sloped gently down into a pool in which we could paddle; another pool upstream was fed by a waterfall and was deep enough for Geoff to swim in. Although small in area, in our imagination this became our very own private beach, better than the seaside, as it was just a few minutes walk from our own back door.

How Stean Gorge.

Further downstream below the How Stean Gorge café and accessible only by crossing a very narrow foot bridge and traversing a slippery and precarious path, high up in the overhanging rock wall of the gorge was a cave, which led back into the hillside emerging under some trees in the middle of one of the fields. This was known as 'Tom Taylor's cave' and so the story goes, many years ago was the hideout of a notorious thief on the run from the law. It was blocked at both ends by locked iron grills at the time, but to us it was so scary that we always kept well away.

Hay-making in summertime would begin with the horse drawn reaper cutting the meadow grass filled with flowers and herbs, which as it dried in the sun gave off the most memorable aroma that continued to carry the smell of summer right through to the freezing days of winter when it was fed to the cows in the byre. The psychological effect of this seemed to lift the temperature several degrees on a cold and frosty winter morning.

All the smells of the countryside seemed pleasant in those days, even the oil liberally applied to the grass cutters, hay turners, and horse-drawn rakes smelled sweet. As the hay dried in the sun it was either turned by a horse-drawn hay turner or very often tossed and shaken out by hand allowing the

Geoff riding on the hay turner.

warm wind to penetrate any thick patches thereby speeding up the drying process. A couple of days later it would be raked into rows so that it could be scooped and piled into heaps by a horse-drawn 'hay sweep', [3] a six foot wide wooden frame with long forward pointing wooden tines which later would be used to scoop up the heaps, dragging them to the barns there to be forked up through a door above the byre. As this was effectively the harvest in the dales all hands were welcome to help and we would happily join in the task of hand turning the hay with the three foot wide wooden peg tined hand rakes.

The reward for our efforts came with the arrival of the 'lowance' [4] delivered in a wicker basket covered with a brightly coloured tea cloth and containing a huge metal pot of sweet milky tea to be drunk from equally large mugs. To complete the feast huge doorstep sized sandwiches of cheese and onion or delicious cold fried bacon and egg were provided. This was consumed while we reclined in the armchair-like comfort of a heap of newly gathered hay. If the field was too far away from the house the pot of tea would be replaced by lemonade bottles filled with cold tea, which was sometimes even more refreshing.

The advantage of storing hay above the animals was that it insulated their winter quarters and feeding was a simple matter of lifting a trapdoor in the floor and dropping the feed down to the cattle below; many of the barns and byres were also conveniently situated in the corners of the fields, avoiding the need to transport hay to the farmstead and the inevitable manure back to the field. Thus, the practicalities of farming in the dales have created their unique beauty.

Preparing for our first winter at Hazel Close involved stocking up the pantry with as much tinned food as rationing permitted, and this turned out to be a wise move as we were virtually cut off by deep snow drifts for nearly six weeks. Even then hours of pleasure and adventure were possible due to the skill of Mr Holmes the village joiner and wheelwright, who made us wooden sledges shod with iron runners that were so well made that they survived back in Ganstead for many years beyond the end of the war. Almost everywhere there was a suitable place for sledging, but the favourite was a field down the side of Middlesmoor hill, however in this case stopping before hitting the dry stone wall at the bottom was frequently a problem.

The very steep road up to the village also featured prominently in the early days of our time there. As I recall Mum and Geoff had been to the village shop for groceries and had put some potatoes, vegetables and me in a pram. Geoff was holding the handle as we descended the steep 'one in four' bank, when apparently and for which I never received a satisfactory explanation, he let go of the handle. Perhaps it was to demonstrate the effect of gravity on a wheeled vehicle without brakes on a steep hill, as a result of which, a pram, a bag of potatoes and one small boy promptly accelerated away. Things took a literal turn for the worse when the Silver Cross pram and I achieved terminal velocity and arrived at a sharp bend in the road. The inherent instability caused by 'T'owd Fat Man', two stone of spuds and a vehicle designed primarily for strolls in the park, resulted in the inevitable shedding of me and the vegetables onto the grass verge Miraculously I was retrieved undamaged from the scene of the crash, and the provisions safely gathered up, though not necessarily in that order of priority.

One concession to food rationing of which we took full advantage was the Ministry of Foods permission to form 'pig clubs' in which a pig could be reared and fattened on kitchen scraps, 'for the consumption of members of the club.' Eventually the day came when our pig was to be butchered. Such an important event was witnessed by us all and we boys were offered its inflated bladder for use as a football; from that very day on I have never been particularly interested in football. Conversely my experience of speed on four wheels in the incident with the pram had the opposite effect and attracted me to fast cars and all things mechanical. As it was mid-summer when the pig was shared out, all its various parts had to be processed the same day for preservation. Mum and Auntie Marge had therefore to make brawn, and they also made sausages and cured a side of bacon, all with very little previous experience. No doubt the pages of Mrs Beeton's cookbook [5] came in very useful, as traditionally every part 'except the squeal' was to be used.

Everybody knows it is very difficult for small boys to avoid getting into mischief occasionally, and so it came to pass that one day in our constant search for adventure, Mike climbed into a horse-drawn farm cart which Neil had left in the yard. I thought it would be a good idea to lift the shafts and pretend to be the horse. What we did not appreciate was that the cart was on a hill and the shafts resting on the ground were the only things preventing it from rolling away. They were not very heavy because a feature of these carts is that the body almost balances on its two large wheels, so the minute I lifted the shafts it started to move. Mike just had time to jump out before it careered to the end of the yard and over a drop of about four feet. Over the edge it flew, miraculously without turning over, but alas it then sped across the field to smash into the stone wall at the bottom. We stood rooted to the spot wondering just how we were going to get out of this little escapade; fortunately the wall was substantial enough to prevent it breaking through and plunging into the gorge. Just how this had happened was going to take a lot of explaining to Neil.

As expected Neil was not best pleased when he discovered that his cart was not where he had left it, nor was it in its original condition; his good nature must have been severely tested and he gave us the telling off we surely deserved. Wisely we put our visits to the cow byre at milking time on hold for a few days and when we did venture back, were very relieved only to be squirted with milk rather than have the bucket thrown at us.

The scale of the surroundings as viewed through our eyes provided endless opportunities for play; to us the narrow tracks across the fields which had been formed by the constant passage of sheep over the years, were our make-believe roads to market or paths to some other figment of our fertile imagination. Even small undulations unnoticed by adults could be turned into bicycle speedways or secret valleys and mountains; in one field a long meandering depression that may have been gouged out by boulders during the Ice Age, became in our eyes a river, and our tricycles magically transformed into Red Indian canoes.

A favourite and harmless pastime involved riding our tricycles up the fields to the roadside, to collect imaginary dog food for our equally imaginary dogs. I cannot recall how many 'dogs' we pretended to have, but judging by the frequency of our journeys they must have been a hungry lot. One day we arrived at the roadside gate to find two fat sacks emblazoned with the words 'DOG FOOD'.

The gate today, though no dog food now.

Fearful of terrible retribution if they were not ours, we circled the sacks like bees round a honey pot, when eventually excitement overcame our fear and we loaded one sack onto each bike and sped downhill at breakneck speed with loud and melodious cries of 'We've got some dog food'! This would show those disbelieving adults that our dogs really did exist.

What we didn't know was that my Dad had come up from Hull for the weekend and had arranged the surprise. As his visits involved him using various modes of transport, a mixture of buses, trains, and sometimes a considerable walk as the bus from Pateley only came up to Middlesmoor on Saturdays, stopping on other days at Lofthouse further down the dale. He must have brought the sacks with him from home but where he found the material for filling them is a mystery.

At that time we did not have a car, until the day Mum attended an auction sale in Pateley and mistakenly but successfully bid for the wrong lot, instantly becoming the very surprised owner of a maroon and black Triumph Eight. Not being able to drive she had to ask the auctioneer if he could deliver it to Hazel Close. Though very small, this old car was to serve us very well for many years after we returned home at the end of the war, but its value initially was that it provided Dad with a more convenient form of transport when visiting us, subject of course to the availability of petrol which was strictly rationed.

Despite such wartime restrictions the Grouse Season [6] continued to attract shooting parties to Nidderdale and for this a vehicle based on a much modified Austin Sixteen saloon car, had been fitted with two gearboxes joined end to end, giving it very low gears for climbing the steepest parts of the moor. Snow chains on the drive wheels for extra grip meant it could literally go anywhere. Christened 'The Jeep' it conveyed many important people up the dale and on to the very top of the moor. Geoff by this time was old enough to go grouse beating [7] for the shooting parties and on one memorable occasion returned from a day on the moors looking rather glum. Mum asked him if he had had a good day, to which he replied, 'No! I had to sit on someone's knee in the jeep'. 'Who was it? she asked. 'Somebody called Tom Walls I think', complained Geoff, at which point both Mum and Auntie Marge cried in unison, 'Tom Walls, the film star?!' This did not impress Geoff one bit as sitting on anyone's knee, even that of a film star was an affront to his dignity.

Geoff also got to ride one of the ponies when beating, and as a treat one day, Mike and I hitched a ride on the back of a particularly sturdy little pony. With three of us on board, myself as the tail end Charlie sitting at the back, the omens were not good.

Starting off from outside the Crown Hotel in the village, we got just past the joiners shop at the top end of the village and through the gate on the track up on to the moor when I slid backwards off the pony to be deposited most unceremoniously in the mud, or in the local jargon I 'tumbled and kiss t'floor',[8] that was as near as I ever got to going grouse beating.

The Crown Hotel, Middlesmoor.

Although we were fairly remote from the war, from time to time there were reminders of it in the shape of stray barrage balloons, one that had broken away from their moorings and drifted overhead, landing on the top

15

of a distant moor. Unlike at home in Hull, Geoff's tin of shrapnel fragments was not added to at all during the four-and-a-half years at Middlesmoor, similarly his note book of airplanes he had spotted remained unfilled beyond the first page of entries.

Although I do not remember it myself Geoff recalls the day a Lancaster bomber flew down the valley, so low that from the village he was actually looking down on it, and that the noise of the engines was absolutely deafening as it flew by only a few feet higher than the chimney pots of Hazel Close, to skim over Gouthwaite reservoir and its dam. He assumes it had first flown over both the Angram and Scarr House reservoirs higher up the valley and then taken a 90° turn to swoop down onto Gouthwaite which has two dam-top towers similar to the ones later attacked in the Dambusters raids in May 1943 on the Möhne and Edersee Dams in the Ruhr in Germany. As it only happened once he thinks it must have been decided that the area was unsuitable for training purposes using the Derwent Reservoirs in Derbyshire instead.

Mike and I were old enough now to attend the village school, and my memories are of writing with chalk on small wooden framed slates, and of Miss Ridley, the headmistress, who taught the big boys and girls in the larger of the two class rooms. Our teacher was Miss Metcalf. Though a very small school, its record of success in sending pupils on to grammar schools was outstanding, and it was from here that Geoff won a scholarship to Ripon Grammar School, though as our eventual return to Ganstead was pending he obtained a transfer to Beverley Grammar school.

We walked up the hill to school each day and in winter this required that we be muffled up in several layers of clothing to the point where I was twice my normal girth and looked like a miniature Scott of the Antarctic. Incidentally, this was quite appropriate as Titus Oates had served in the West Yorkshire Regiment garrisoned in York. He is remembered for his immortal last words on the ill-fated expedition to the South Pole: 'I am just going outside and may be some time'. He was never seen alive again.

We were allowed one hour for dinner and in this time it was just possible for us to run down the hill to Hazel Close for a hurried meal and be back at school before one o'clock, for failure to beat the clock meant having to face Miss Ridley, not a happy fate.

Sadly during our third winter at Hazel Close Grandma died and was buried at Middlesmoor Church. Although it was sad, it is hard to imagine a more beautiful last resting place, with its incredible view the length of Nidderdale, over Lofthouse to Gouthwaite reservoir and a distant Pateley Bridge. We often took the path from the church, walking down the concrete steps that must have been hollow because they echoed each and every step of our leather, steel nailed clogs, to such an extent that you felt you would be heard far down below in Lofthouse village.

The timeless view of Nidderdale from the Church.

Intriguingly despite its remoteness there must have been plans ultimately to defend the village, and this came to light one day when Mike and I were walking home from school down to the bottom of the hill and decided on a short cut across the fields. Climbing over the gate we were curious to see what was in a shed barely visible from the road as it was cut into the steep bank on the edge of a wood. Peering through a crack in the padlocked wooden doors we couldn't believe our eyes. Pointing straight at us was the barrel of a large army field gun. We were old enough to have heard the constant reminders that 'careless talk costs lives', and knew this gun was meant to be a secret and we shouldn't know that it was there, so I didn't tell anybody what we had seen until well after the war had ended. Its position with a direct line of fire down the dale would have been ideal, but what was it defending other than a remote dales village? Could it be that as the road below controlled access to the Scar and Angram reservoirs, vital for supplying water to towns like Bradford and Leeds, and following the damage the R.A.F. had inflicted on the German war effort by destroying such facilities in Germany, the Government's sensitivity to their protection must have been very high indeed.

As it is now, without doors or a gun.

1 A form of gelatin.

2 Yorkshire dialect meaning 'The Old'.

3 A six foot wide wooden frame with long forward pointing wooden tines dragged by a horse to gather rows of hay into heaps.

4 Otherwise known as the allowance; the mid-morning or mid-afternoon refreshment for farm workers in the field.

5 *Beeton's Book of Household Management* was a guide to all aspects of running a household in Victorian Britain, edited by Isabella Beeton. It was originally entitled *Beeton's Book of Household Management*, in line with the other guide-books published by Beeton. Previously published as a part work, it was first published as a book in 1861 by S. O. Beeton Publishing, 161 Bouverie Street, London, a firm founded by her husband, Samuel Beeton. See: http://en.wikipedia.org/wiki/Mrs_Beeton%27s_Book_of_Household_Management

6 The Grouse Season, often referred to as 'The Glorious Twelfth' commences annually on 12th August.

7 Walking across the moor to drive the grouse up into the air and towards the guns.

8 Fell face down on to the floor.

9 A large balloon tethered with a steel cable to deter low flying enemy aircraft.

10 Splintered pieces of bombs or shells.

2
Return to Ganstead

As the war drew towards an end in 1945 the time came to go back to our home in Ganstead and to a very different environment. Hull had suffered badly from the bombing but fortunately our bungalows survived more or less intact, except for the need to strip and re-plaster the ceilings that had suffered from the vibrations of the bombing. Although Ganstead was not a prime target several enemy pilots had preferred to dump their bombs in the fields and run for home rather than risk being shot down by anti-aircraft fire near the docks; as an encouragement to do this some low lying fields had been flooded so that by moonlight they would be mistaken for the intended target.

The recovery from the war seemed to pose far more problems than the four-and-a-half years we had spent away for there was not the ability to live from the land in the way that we had enjoyed at Hazel Close, and life was generally a much more serious affair. There was also the move to a new school, ten times bigger than tiny Middlesmoor School, and consequently, despite the best efforts of the teachers I do not look back on those school days as the best years of my life, so much so that there are few episodes of any significance that I can recall. I was not keen on team sports so only negative memories remain, such as the occasion when I was called upon at the last minute to play in goal for the school junior football team. As it was an away game football shorts were required instead of the short trousers which had sufficed for sports days. As an emergency measure one of the teachers, Mrs Downing, big hearted with proportions to match, rustled up what I am convinced to this day were a pair of her bloomers which were purple in colour, and if as I suspect had been made of parachute silk would have required a whole parachute.

The team. Author (front row left) with the suspect purple shorts, and Mike (back row right).

My efforts in goal were therefore less than inspiring, retrieving the ball with one hand whilst taking up the slack in the shorts with the other proved a disaster for the team, losing by several goals to nil. My embarrassment was heightened by the fact that both teams and most of the supporters had come to the same conclusion as me as to the origin of my shorts. So ended my mercifully short football career. The alternative of cricket also held little interest for me as I could see no sense in inviting somebody to throw a very hard ball at you with as much murderous intent as he could muster, when all you were given to defend yourself with was a piece of wood four inches wide and about two foot long. Even if you succeeded in hitting the ball you then had to run to the bowler's end but instead of hitting him with the bat in retaliation, you turned around and ran back giving him the opportunity to maim you again. The most enjoyable interludes in my days at Bilton school were the occasions when the headmaster, Mr Fox, took us on walking trips to the Yorkshire dales, the most memorable began with us staying the night at Skipton Youth Hostel. Before walking to the Hostel in Kettlewell the next day, the headmaster made sure that we were all in bed early so as to ensure he could get some peace and quiet in the village pub for the evening. The following day's walk took in Great Wernside and Malham Tarn which fully tested our wet weather gear with torrential rain for a good part of the way. I had been equipped with an ex-army cape which Dad had got from the army surplus store; it was a bell-shaped one piece garment with no arms, the top part went over my head and was made of clear plastic, the rest of the khaki cape extended down over the top of my wellington boots, so was completely waterproof. Unfortunately, a severe problem manifested itself after walking for only a few minutes when my breath completely steamed up the clear plastic top, reducing forward visibility to only what I could see by looking through the open bottom of the cape at my feet and the area of ground about two feet in front of me. In an attempt to travel as light as possible the cape was the only wet weather cover I had so the next few miles were covered with difficulty by walking very close to the person in front and seeing only the back of his heels. Mercifully the rain soon stopped and the rest of the trip was covered in the dry. Mr Fox was such a fan of the dales that the he and his family eventually bought a holiday cottage in Middlesmoor.

Back at school, the best part the day was 'home time' except on occasions when laughter had not succeeded in diffusing an argument and failed to pacify one of the school bullies, this invariably culminated in the threat of 'I'll get you at home-time Taylor.' At these times it was prudent to walk home via a footpath that was accessed through a hole in the fence behind the school, then on through 'Little Wood' across a field to 'Big Wood' where we had tied a rope to an overhanging branch, from which we could swing Tarzan-like across the dyke at this point several yards wide and quite deep, generally though not always, landing on the opposite side without mishap.

The dyke flowed past our bungalows and provided many opportunities for more ambitious schemes one of which involved building a series of dams to create lakes and waterfalls. Unfortunately, one particular spring day, the combination of one of our dams and a week of heavy April showers culminated in the stream backing up through the drains and subsequently flooding neighbouring gardens.

Messing about with water inevitably included building rafts to float on a pond at the farm of school friend Eddie. On one memorable day a raft made from planks of wood and empty oil drums had drifted away from the bank, and our efforts to recover it by throwing bricks and stones were only partially successful, bringing it almost but not quite within reach. I was sure that if I anchored myself by holding onto a conveniently placed fence post with one hand, whilst reaching at full stretch across the water with the other, I should be able to grab the raft and pull it to the side.

Regrettably, the instant my fingertips touched our little craft, the combination of my near horizontal form and a rotten fence post, conspired to deposit me into what proved to be only a few inches of water concealing several feet of black slime, the product of decades of drainage from the cow sheds and middens.[1] Inevitably, I plumbed the depths of this disgusting mixture before surfacing to scramble up the bank, looking like the creature from the black lagoon. There followed a half mile trek home across the fields, first emptying my wellington boots, which proved only of temporary benefit as they slowly filled again with the runoff from my sodden clothes. The trail of squelching footsteps were undeniable evidence pointing to where we had been, so any thoughts of plausible excuses would be futile, in any case it was doubtful if any adult would want to come near enough to me to administer punishment as the smell was pretty overpowering.

Arriving home I thought that a two stage approach might lessen the blow so Auntie Marge's was the first port of call; her reaction was a cry of 'Where have you two been? Stay out there in the yard John and don't move', followed in short order by several bowls of water poured all over me, before being sent home for the second stage of the process. My mother's repeat of the now familiar cry, 'Where have you been? Stay out there in the yard and don't move', but this time followed by the added instruction to 'Get those filthy clothes off now.'

The removal of my clothes attracted another drenching this time by buckets of thankfully slightly warmer water; I think it was considered that pneumonia was probably the least serious sickness that might result from my latest escapade. Once I was sufficiently swilled down to be allowed into the house further surface decontamination took place in the bath, whilst my natural immunity to disease tackled any internal impurities. Needless to say Eddie's pond was then placed firmly out of bounds.

The two bungalows (centre) at Ganstead; ours was the left one
('Eggs for sale' sign in hedge) Mike's is on the right.

As can be seen in the photograph of our bungalows, the two garden lawns together were big enough for a tennis court to be laid out. The L-shaped buildings at the bottom of our garden housed the chickens whose eggs we sold at the door. Mike and I each had bedrooms in the lofts and we found we could climb out of the dormer windows and by carefully negotiating our way around the chimney on the ridge of the roof would end up in each other's bedrooms, much to the consternation of our parents. This practice was curtailed when one wet and slippery night I lost my footing and fell down the roof into our front garden, finally giving the game away when I knocked on our front door in my pyjamas asking to be let in.

A much more life threatening episode involved a couple of 12 bore shotgun cartridges which we found near 'dyke den', which as the name implies was a hide-out under the hedge in a dry dyke. The cartridges were suitable material for a little experiment in which we cut one of them open to expose the gun powder that we then poured into a small hole in the root of a nearby horse-chestnut tree, the lead shot was then piled on top as was the other cartridge, with some paper to ignite the powder. Lighting the paper, we dived for cover into the den, lying flat on the earth floor waiting for the bang, and after what seemed ages there was an almighty explosion sending hundreds of rooks nesting in 'Big Wood' half a mile away, squawking into the air. Peering out of our shelter, the tree emerged from a haze of smoke and falling leaves. In a split second autumn had come for that tree as the lead-shot stripped it of most of its leaves.

It is a wonder we survived some of our escapades, such as the occasion when Mike and I were flying our new box-kites and we discovered that we could make them dive to skim the ground and then be sent soaring back up into the sky. Developing this skill further we dive-bombed each other or more exactly I dive-bombed Mike with my kite, unfortunately knocking one of his teeth out in the process. This was only one of the incidents in which he always seemed to be on the receiving end of a prank which misfired. The next occurred when we were having a pea shooter battle and I fired a pea that firmly and irretrievably stuck in poor Mike's ear, requiring a visit to hospital to have it removed. There was also the unfortunate time when I accidentally hit him on the head with a garden rake. It must have seemed we didn't get on together, but nothing could be further from the truth, we have always been more like brothers than cousins and still are to this day.

Sometimes the accidents happened only to me, like the time in Dad's garage when Mike, Eddie Ogram and I were having a serious discussion about something or other; Mike and Eddie were outside the door and I was swinging by my arms on a roof truss, and I remember saying with all the authority I could muster: 'I think Mr Churchill …' for that's as far as I got when bang! the beam gave way and part of the garage roof came down around me. As a consequence of this the electricity cable from the house to the garage parted leaving the bare ends dangling down and from which I received an enormous electric shock that luckily threw me backwards away from further danger. I never finished that sentence so Mike and Eddie never knew what words of pearl-like wisdom they should have received. The least said the better of the time we (accidentally) set fire to our neighbour's hedge – we didn't know that gorse was so flammable.

Less destructive ways of spending my time included helping on the nearby farm, usually this involved loading turnips from the field into a horse-drawn cart and forking them through a trapdoor high in the barn wall where they subsequently would roll down a chute into the turnip cutter ready for mixing with chaff [2] and rolled barley for feeding to cows and horses. Once I had proved reasonably capable, Mr Holly whose task this normally was, let me harness the horse 'Captain,' hitch him to the cart and go on my own down to the field. Once, when due to an error on my part, the cart wheel gave the gate post a hefty nudge as we left the yard, Captain then took charge and ignored my tugs on the reins. He was so used to the daily routine that he plodded unerringly down the track into the turnip field and stopped at the end of the next row ready for loading, moving forward as and when required without further instruction from me.

Thanks to Captain's years of experience we were to perform this operation many times during the school holidays, and at the end of the week Mr Holly would give me sixpence, which at a time when his weekly wage would only be about four pounds was very generous, especially as I would have willingly done it all for nothing.

1 A dump for domestic waste of all kinds.
2 Corn husks and chopped up pieces of straw, sometimes referred to as 'Kaf'.

3

Holidays in Scarborough

Summer holidays were spent in Scarborough and began with the loading of the trusty Triumph's rear luggage rack with a cabin trunk containing our clothes surmounted by a large tin trunk that was packed with as much food as Mum had been able to collect during the preceding weeks, only restricted by the limits of wartime food rationing. The only food at the B&B would be what we could provide or for what we had the coupons.

Not only was the poor little car expected to carry this load of luggage but also Mum and Dad in the front, and Grandpa, Geoff and I somehow squeezed onto the back seat; it clawed its way slowly up some very steep hills between Bridlington and Scarborough. A special technique was developed on the steepest parts of the journey which involved us all pushing forward in our seats, employing a rocking motion of the body, but with more energy put into the rock forward than the gentle lean back. A similar action as is used to activate a playground swing. This was then reinforced by chants of 'Come on little car', 'You can do it, you can do it', and 'I think you can, I think you can', culminating at the top of the hill with 'I thought you could, I thought you could.' Well it worked for us.

We stayed at the boarding house home of Mr and Mrs Wintle, conveniently situated overlooking Peasholme Park, through which we walked every morning down to the beach. Our accommodation was on a bed and breakfast basis with the welcome addition of the Sunday lunch. For this longed for treat we handed over the required coupons to cover the ingredients for a sumptuous roast beef, roast potatoes and two veg, before which as a first course in line with tradition we feasted on probably the best Yorkshire puddings in the county. They were the size of a dinner plate and of sufficient depth to hold a good half a pint of mouth-watering onion gravy.

Mrs Wintle was a very large lady whilst Mr Wintle was tiny by comparison; they never called each other by their Christian names, it was always 'Mr Wintle, will you do this', and the reply would invariably be 'Very good Mrs Wintle.' This formal way of addressing each other was not uncommon in those days, consequently I never discovered their Christian names.

Most of our meals were prepared and eaten in the beach chalet that we rented on the North Bay. These small wooden beach huts contained a fold down table and four chairs plus a tiny cooker known as a 'Baby Belling'. As the electricity was free it doubled as a room heater if you left the oven door open with it switched on, a boon on the occasional cold or wet and stormy days. This was invaluable as we were not allowed back to the 'digs' [1] during the day, and were not permitted to stay in the chalets after 10.00 p.m.

(left) The author, mother, father and brother, Geoff in Chalet Number 36, North Bay; (right) The author and his mother.

It was some time before signs of war were completely removed from the seafront, with huge 10 ton blocks of concrete preventing access to the Marine Drive other than on foot. Many of the hotels had been requisitioned to accommodate troops and it was not unusual to see army jeeps lined up in a hotel car park. American and Canadian soldiers occupied the Dorchester hotel opposite the Wintle's house for some time after the end of hostilities.

Like most children all we wanted was sea, sand and sun, but could be just as happy on a wild and stormy day, sitting in a deckchair in the shelter of the chalet, wrapped in thick warm rugs watching huge waves batter the sea wall, shooting spray twenty or thirty feet into the air and soaking anybody standing too close to the edge.

On at least one evening of the holiday we would go to a show at the Floral Hall, best described as a greenhouse with a stage. The whole building was full of plants with ivy entwined around the pillars and trailed across the roof. The garden atmosphere was enhanced by numerous birds, which had found their way inside and made their nests amongst the foliage, engaging in 'bombing runs' on the audience.

Apart from these shows the cost of the holiday over and above what we would spend living at home was limited to bed and Sunday lunch, plus the rent of the beach chalet. We provided the rest of the food ourselves, generally from the copious depths of the essential black tin trunk. Even so it must have required careful budgeting and saving throughout the year by Mum and Dad when eventually we were able to spend the last three weeks of August and the first week of September (Scarborough Cricket Festival Week) on holiday. Given my lack of enthusiasm for the game of cricket this last week was primarily for Dad's benefit, needless to say we never complained at the chance of another week on the beach.

Early each year I began to save threepenny bits for spending money on the summer holidays, which in the early years were primarily used to buy additions to my Hornby Dublo train set. One much sought after item was a 'High Capacity Wagon', a long four axle eight wheel articulated goods wagon that used up quite few of the little hexagonal bronze coins. Paddling canoes on Peasholme Park boating lake or swimming in the North Bay Pool then competed with treacle covered waffles or ice cream for a share of the precious funds.

Over the years we met and made many friends, renting adjoining chalets for the same weeks each year, for this was the only time we all met in the twelve months, and when friendships were renewed. A feature for the men was the evening 'domino school' held in one of the chalets. For the children, when the tide was out and the beach had emptied of people heading back to their hotels for tea, we would troop down onto the virtually deserted sands for a game of cricket. This was the only time I ever enjoyed playing cricket and will never forget those games, and the patience of a very kind Mr Gibbins who organised them.

Each year I eagerly awaited the arrival of the Gibbins family, particularly their daughter Molly, eventually plucking up the courage to ask her out to the pictures. I think this took me several years to do, or maybe it just seemed like several years, but I bet it was the only time she was ever taken out for the evening by someone who paid for the tickets in threepenny bits. If ever a boy knew how to impress a girl it certainly wasn't me. Less heart-throbbing moments comprised a solitary but very relaxing pastime floating gently for an hour or more, rocking on the waves in my bright yellow ex-R.A.F. rubber-dinghy, safely secured from drifting away from land by a sea anchor. I would be content to do this until eventually the sun disappeared behind the cliff top and it was time to begin the trek back through Peasholme Park to the Wintle's.

From time to time each year a man would come down to the beach and build some very impressive sculptures in the sand, collecting donations from holiday makers, tossed into his strategically placed bucket. He created everything from elephants to cars or ships and some very elaborate castles.

By comparison my efforts at sand castle building were pretty un-impressive, until one day when I excelled myself, constructing a very fine castle, which looked as though it may even survive the ravages of the incoming tide. With this in mind I sat within its ramparts confidently waiting for the imminent victory of man against the forces of nature. Somewhat less confidently I suspect, Geoff sat in a deckchair in front of the chalet watching the proceedings, at this precise moment a youth about twice my age and size ran along the beach jumping with both feet onto my work of art, and destroying it completely.

For a few seconds I sat there in disbelief. It is said that people with red hair have a fiery temperament, only requiring the tripping of a hair-trigger before reacting. On this occasion the trigger was pulled by Geoff, who shouted at the top of his voice, 'Go get him John', very much as a shepherd would command a sheep dog. My stunned anger was instantly transformed into rage and in a split second I was on my feet chasing down the perpetrator of the crime, in shepherding terms this is known as 'the fetch'. Catching up with him the 'sheepdog' turned into a 'panther', throwing myself onto his back and bringing him down into the sand, then setting about him with justifiably indignant fury. Fortunately for both of us Geoff arrived on the scene to separate us before the youth recovered and realised that he was only being attacked by someone less than half his size.

1 Slang for a boarding house or rented place of dwelling.

4
What shall I be?

A defining moment as a teenager comes when you are first asked, 'What do you want to be when you leave school'? I remember trying to think of something involving a minimum amount of reading, writing, or arithmetic, I was convinced that I was not very clever. But the answer had been implanted in me without me realising it during those formative years in Nidderdale. It was obvious. 'I would be a farmer.'

We had kept a few chickens at the bottom of the garden for our own eggs and decided to build a hen house and wire netting run for about sixty laying hens with a view to selling fresh eggs at the door. Second-hand timber that was readily available from the demolition of bomb damaged buildings in Hull, always smelt of burning and brick dust. Dad seemed to know where to find it and some asbestos sheets which he bought and arranged for them to be delivered on the horse-drawn cart of the Hull to Hornsea carrier.

Soon a suitable building was constructed and day-old chicks were ordered from a hatchery in Easingwold, these were collected from Hull Station a few days later. They were introduced to their new quarters and kept warm under infra-red heat lamps until they were big enough to face the world without artificial heat.

Eventually they grew old enough to begin to lay the long-awaited eggs and before long they were producing fifty to sixty eggs per day, our roadside sign proclaiming 'Fresh Eggs 1s/6d a Dozen' was drawing in passers-by at a rate which sometimes meant eggs were so fresh they were still warm as the customers took them away. Indeed a visit to the nest boxes was often required to make up a full dozen. As we were the first premises selling fresh eggs on the road out of town the operation was a huge success. So much so that a year later a neighbour two doors away copied our building design even erecting an identical sign to ours on the roadside in front of his house. Though there was sufficient demand for both of us he started by dropping his price by a penny below ours, totally unnecessary as we continued to sell all we produced, he would watch us chalking our price on the board in the morning and immediately rush out to adjust his price accordingly.

In 1950, the opportunity came to take the entrance examination for Hull College of Technology 'building department'. It was thought this would provide education opportunities not available at primary schools, whilst learning manual skills in joinery, technical drawing, plumbing and bricklaying. Passing the examination I was called for a formal interview prior to being offered a place.

As a family we were taught that you must always tell the truth. And on this occasion the interview was going very well until I was asked which sector of the building industry I was primarily interested in? 'Farming' was my honest but disastrous reply. Undaunted, I sat the examination again the following year, once more attending the interview. By now a little older and a lot wiser, my response to the infamous question was that I was hoping to gain wide experience in all sectors. A salutary lesson in interview technique: tell them only what they want to hear without too much detail and you don't have to tell lies to succeed.

The down side of becoming a Tech' College student in Osborne Street manifested itself in the form of a pair of very itchy grey flannel trousers. The blazer and cap were fine but my legs were much more accustomed to shorts and had over the years of exposure become capable of withstanding nettle stings and even barbed wire, but not the constant abrasive scratching due to being enclosed in the obligatory long grey flannels. The smart new uniform soon developed the patina of use, helped in this respect by the tradition of locking new boys in the outside toilets and tipping copious amounts of very dusty boiler house coal over the top of the door.

There were no facilities for school meals and most students either took packed lunches or bought fish and chips or meat pies in the town cafés. Lunch break lasted an hour and a quarter, therefore it was just possible to run and catch the bus home, eat a very quick hot dinner and get back to Osborne Street with about five minutes to spare. This feat was made possible by the fact that buildings which may have impeded my direct route to the bus stop had been destroyed during the war leaving open bomb-sites.

The procedure was that the bus left the terminus at 12.05 p.m. and took about three minutes to reach the nearest stop on George Street; if I got out of the class on time it took four minutes to run to the stop. The journey to Ganstead took twenty minutes so I could be in the house by 12.30 p.m., fifteen minutes to eat my dinner and catch the 12.45 p.m. bus back into town, arriving at George Street at 1.05 p.m. and the school door with five minutes to spare. It was worth all this effort to get out of the town and into the countryside, not forgetting the advantage of a good hot dinner each day. A bus pass enabled me to travel as many times as I liked at no extra cost.

A good proportion of school work involved the practical side and we were taught bricklaying, plumbing, and joinery, all of which I found very interesting. Though most of my classmates would go on to enter the building trade in one form or another the skills that I gained were to prove equally valuable during a farming career as we built many of our farm buildings and eventually our two homes.

There were a multitude of unique characters both in and out of school, providing opportunities for the pranksters amongst us. The joinery teacher Mr Bray had a keen interest in stocks and shares and every morning would stand at the main door of the school while we all filed past into lessons, and under his arm would be the day's issue of the *Financial Times*, recognisable by its pink paper. The polite greeting of 'Good morning Sir', to which was added 'Can I borrow your Sporting Pink', invariably resulted in the offending youth receiving a clout across the head with the rolled up newspaper and his reply of 'This is not a sporting pink boy it is the *Financial Times*.' By the time we had all filed in and the swatting process had been repeated several times, Sir's paper was in shreds and the school steps had become littered with pink confetti.

In the practical joinery lessons Mr Bray had a particular trait in that almost everything we made included the measurement 'One inch and seven eighths by seven eighths'. It would not have been surprising if we had all gone through life producing nothing but buildings entirely constructed in units of 'One inch and seven eighths by seven eighths' So important was this to him that terrible retribution befell anyone who challenged its sanctity, this retribution could strike without warning often in the shape of a wood chisel thrown with merciful skill, to embed itself in the offending students work-bench probably missing him by precisely 'One inch and seven eighths'.

Two of the characters out of school were Smokey Joe and Eva Smith, or Eva Brick as we called her due to her propensity for hurling lumps of brick rubble at hapless passers-by. Joe on the other hand seemed harmless enough as he shuffled around in his permanent attire of tattered trousers and all-weather string vest. He was engaged in a constant search for discarded cigarette tab-ends, taking liquid refreshment from a bottle the contents of which may well have been equally at home in a primus stove.

Eva may have been fuelled by similar concoctions that no doubt explained why one day she entered the school yard, preceded by a bread loaf which she had been kicking along the street. Thinking that she was treating it as a football it was dutifully kicked back; this action met with a string of abuse and a brick from Eva as she picked up the loaf, tearing off a chunk to eat before continuing out of the yard and along the street.

The majority of students went on to pursue successful careers as tradesmen, builders, and architects, or even property developers. My aim in 1953 was still to be a farmer, leaving school to work on a small dairy and poultry farm five miles down the road from home.

My job had become vacant when the previous youth had left to join the army to serve two years National Service, which in my case had been deferred for two years whilst I was employed in agriculture. As it transpired conscription for National Service was discontinued before the day of my eventual call-up came, and my request to join the Royal Air Force was never answered. Fortunately for the safety of the realm it never reached the point of such desperation as to warrant a call on my services.

The farm I worked on comprised thirty acres in a long narrow strip, made up for its lack of land by employing what were then some very new intensive methods. The poultry unit produced day-old chicks for sale to rearing and egg producing farms, eggs were incubated in a highly automated hatchery and transported in special boxes by road and rail all over England.

To keep thirty cows on thirty acres also required new ideas, so during the summer the land was fenced off into small paddocks each sufficient to feed the cows for a week. Each morning while the cowman Jack was milking I would go down to the field and move an electric fence a couple of yards further onto the un-grazed area providing that day's fresh feed for the returning herd. As the grass was nearly always wet with morning dew water gradually spread up my wellington boots leading to wet and sore knees. To avoid this I soon learned to walk with my feet and knees further apart, it is this necessary habit and not horse riding which makes most farmers slightly bow legged.

On a farm like this one you had to be pretty strong as most work involved lifting heavy objects and in those days there were no regulations restricting how much you should lift or carry. In fact there was a fair amount of competition among us as to what we could carry. A typical boast was, 'I once knew a man who could stand in a bushel scuttle [1] and lift himself off the ground'. One of the men, Johnny Wayne (not the film star) used to carry the tarpaulin stack sheet up a ladder onto the top of a stack of sheaves of corn. When it had not been finished and thatched by the evening, when wet this sheet weighed about twenty stone (127kg) whereas he himself probably only weighed about twelve stone (76kg).

Harvesting the corn was by binder as combines were few and far between in the early days. On this farm the binder had originally been pulled by three horses but had been converted by the village blacksmith to be pulled by a tractor. Its purpose was to cut the corn and tie it into sheaves which were deposited in rows across the field. My job was to take six rows wide and bring the sheaves together into stooks of twelve. It was important to line each stook with the ends pointing north and south so that through the day the sun would shine equally on both sides of the stook drying all twelve sheaves. Johnny Wayne usually drove the tractor and kept in the toolbox the head of a claw hammer, which as he reached the final piece of the crop, he would stand up in his seat watching for rabbits to run out. That was when the hammer head came into play as with unerring accuracy he would throw it for an outright kill and one for the pot as he would say.

Loading by forking the stooks up on to a trailer required adherence to certain rules. Depending on what part of the operation he was performing the man on the trailer would shout to the forkers either 'Shipping' or 'Binding'. Shipping meant he wanted to receive them with the bottom of the sheaf to the outside of the trailer, binding meant he wanted the ends inward; if you got it wrong he may well throw them back at you. The same process would be repeated as you unloaded the trailer onto the stack.

Ploughing in those days required a dead straight furrow with all stubble and green material buried, in fact an old saying was: 'You should be able to stand in the furrow at one end of the field and see your boots when looking back from the other end.'

When it came to thrashing the stack the worst job of all would be given to the youngest lad who for a time was me; this was the job of chaff carrying. In my first introduction to it I was given two large old hessian sacks and told to cut them up along one side and the bottom, and then stitch them together to make a chaff sheet which would then be about eight feet square. This was then placed at the side of the thrashing machine near a chute which blew most the dust and chaff on to the sheet and the rest into my face, mouth, ears in fact any orifice it could find. Barley was the worst crop for this as the bristly barley awns [2] get into your clothing, boots and socks. Once piled up on the sheet you would pull all four corners together and twist them tight, whilst in one motion swinging it up onto your shoulder and back so that from behind all that could be seen was a big sack with feet. It then had to be carried up the granary steps to be tipped on to a heap before you heard the shout of 'Where is that b****y kaf lad, it's piling up here already.'

Whilst all this was happening in my life, Geoff had left Beverley Grammar School and worked away from home on a farm at North Dalton near Driffield for two years, leaving to spend a year at Askham Bryan Agricultural College before returning to the same farm. Cousin Mike had completed his National Service in the army and returned to work as an auto-electrical engineer in Hull.

1 A tub-like container for measuring corn by volume.
2 Brittle whisker-like appendage of barley that can appear in other corn crops.

5

We bought a Farm

Mum and Dad however were keen to see us farming in our own right and we began looking for a small farm to buy, scouring the advertisements in the *Yorkshire Post*, looking at places the length and breadth of the county. Each visit was followed by hours of calculating and planning, working out if and how we could afford to buy, usually coming to the conclusion that the problems were insurmountable and the money could not be raised.

There were so many costs to take into account, not only the purchase price of the farm, but the cost of livestock and feed or seeds and fertiliser, most of which would not show a return until the first harvest. The need to buy a tractor and other machinery only added to the daunting challenge we faced. After several years of hopes and the ensuing disappointments, a forty acre farm came onto the market just one mile away across the fields from home.

Hill Farm at Thirtleby, though visible from my bedroom window, was a mile down a narrow lane off the main road at Coniston, and despite being so near it was a lane we had never been down in nearly twenty years of living at Ganstead. Once again and for the umpteenth time we did the inevitable calculations spreading the front room floor with sheets of paper covered in calculations. The asking price was £100.00 an acre, £40,000 in total; this had the advantage of being considered by competing buyers as far too dear for them to even consider, giving us some time to come up with an offer where in the past we had been quickly out-bid by more wealthy opposition.

As the farm was only a couple of miles away by road Mum and Dad agreed that the only answer was to sell their house and for all of us to move to Hill Farm; this was quite a sacrifice for Mum as she had lived in her beloved bungalow at Ganstead most of her married life. Dad didn't seem to mind or at least if he did, he didn't ever show it.

The owner of the farm was a Miss Elliott who had let most of the land to the next door farm in Thirtleby. The house and buildings, which had no electricity and had only recently been connected to the mains water supply, previously drawing water by an outside pump from a brick-lined well in the garden, was at the time being rented by a man who worked as a night watchman in a Hull factory. He kept chickens and ducks in some of the buildings, which though solidly built, were in dire need of cleaning out. A barn was full of bundles of very stiff sweeping brush bristles, also barrels of tar and lengths of timber drilled with rows of holes. The reason for this strange collection was his side line, which involved making sweeping brush heads to sell to ironmongers.

Hill Farm, Thirtleby, 1956.

Miss Elliott's brother was handling the sale of the farm and Geoff visited him in his house in Willerby to negotiate the purchase. The outcome was better than we could ever have expected, to the effect that if we agreed the price and paid a small deposit he would provide a private mortgage at a very reasonable rate, and we need pay only the interest until such time as we could afford to pay off the capital. This would enable us to use some of the proceeds from the sale of Mum and Dad's bungalow to buy milking cows, and generate at least some income fairly quickly.

It is fair to say that without the help and faith of our parents and the deal struck with Mr Elliott and many other people we were to do business with later, we would never have become farmers, certainly not ones owning our own farm.

In April 1956, we at last gained possession of the land and access to the house, enabling us to install electricity instead of oil lamps for lighting, and hot running water replacing the coal-fired boiler in what had euphemistically been called the bathroom. Removing the huge brick and cast iron boiler left space for a proper W.C. and released the outside privy to become a coal house and firewood store. Much later when oil was only fifty pence per gallon, or about eleven pence per litre, we were able to install oil-fired central heating throughout the house. My period of education at building college began to pay off as we did the whole installation ourselves.

6
Taylor Brothers, Farmers

Most importantly a milking parlour complete with milking machines and a dairy were needed before cows could be bought to provide the monthly milk cheque on which we would rely for a regular income. In the meantime I would continue to work at Old Hall Farm in Ganstead and we would share my wages. Only eleven acres were down to grass when we moved in so it was not going to be possible to carry a large herd but we had to start somewhere, and that monthly milk cheque was essential.

Geoff started to work on the buildings making them fit to house livestock. Part of the barn was cleaned out and the yard area fenced off using steel gates bought from a dealer who toured the farms every year in a battered old Ford van, which wasn't long enough for the gates and half of which always hung out of the back. This made the front of the van so light that I am sure if his wife, who could best be described as a 'huge asset', ever got out to stretch her legs, the whole thing would tip over backwards.

All deals were for cash of course and as he was of very slight build she took charge of the money and effectively rode 'shotgun'. She had the kind of presence, that if you made the mistake of looking her in the eye whilst negotiating discount with her husband, it had you immediately fumbling in your pocket eager to pay the full asking price. These gates were cheap but effective, cunningly constructed in such a way that they would usually only

The author, his brother Geoff, and Duke the sheep dog in 1959.
To the left of the post box in the wall is the windscreen of the author's Jeep.

last until about a week before his next annual visit.

Various farm sales produced secondhand milking machines and a new in-churn cooler, which fitted on to the top of a churn and circulated cold tap water through pipes submerged into the milk before running down the outside of the churn, a cheap but efficient system. Stalls for four cows were built into the small brick building and an adjacent barn was made into a dairy. With the pipe work and electric vacuum pump installed we were ready to start a herd.

For this we had available the princely sum of £500.00 to purchase suitable stock. Geoff's former boss Dick Wright agreed to join him for moral support at the cattle auction at Otley market, noted for its sales of good quality dairy cows. After careful scrutiny of the sales catalogue various promising beasts were selected, culminating in five good milking cows being bought for £100.00 each. With his funds now depleted totally and nothing left to pay a haulier to transport his purchases home, Geoff sought out the sellers for some 'luck money'. [1] This is a farming tradition and on this occasion was an absolute necessity, but unfortunately only raised £5.00, not enough to pay a haulier. Dick came to the rescue paying for a cattle wagon to take the cows to Thirtleby before collecting a load of sheep from his farm near Driffield to deliver back to York on the return journey.

As we had not known how many, or if any cows would be arriving, Geoff rushed home and made a last minute dash to Hull to collect some milk churns from Clover Dairies and arrange for their collection the next day. It was early evening when the lorry pulled into the yard and unloaded the five Friesians, which by this time were well overdue for their afternoon milking. They proved very reluctant to enter the strange new surroundings of our very small milking parlour that only accommodated four cows at a time, however the offer of substantial quantities of cattle nuts soon had them contentedly munching away probably relieved to be milked at last. Initially we only had enough grass to support the five cows as the twenty-five acre field and four acres half a mile away had been sown with wheat by the previous tenant. The cows grazed the seven acre field across the lane and the four acre paddock next to the house. The regular cheque from the Milk Marketing Board on the 21st of every month was vital to us.

Equally valuable were Dad's connections in the seed trade, one example was his contact with the manager of the local seed and animal feed firm Barkers & Lee Smith, who agreed to supply us with seed, fertiliser and cattle feed with up to nine months interest free credit, payable when we could afford it or when the arable crop was harvested. Without such faith and trust we would have found things financially very difficult. We endeavoured to repay his generosity by loyally trading with him for almost thirty years until his retirement, including several years after Barkers was taken over by the farming co-operative Brandsby Agricultural Trading Association, where he became the financial director.

A friend of the family, Syd Bays, who had used one of his lorries to move us to Middlesmoor years ago, also stepped in to help. He asked Frank Hill, one of his auctioneer friends to buy five in-pig gilts at the market, send him the bill, and have them delivered to us, telling us we could pay him when we had sold the resulting litters of piglets. Such generosity was a godsend to us at a crucial time. It may have been a coincidence but there were just five pens for them when they arrived.

After harvest we attended a sale of farm machinery in Wansford, successfully bidding for an American Case tractor and a plough, enabling us to cultivate the land in preparation for sowing the following spring. Autumn proved exceptionally wet that year and before we could begin ploughing the field became waterlogged and flooded for half its length. There was no alternative but to press on, with the water in places almost covering the tractor front wheels; we were literally ploughing under water and at times could not see the completed furrows. When it got dark the tractor, with no such refinements as lights, could clearly be seen illuminated by the white-hot glow from the exhaust as it traversed back and forth across the field.

A winter of severe frosts led inevitably to spring and the time to sow a crop of barley. The frosts had done the job of crumbling down the soil, an absolutely essential prerequisite on Holderness clay. Several passes with a set of harrows weighted down with blocks of concrete eventually provided a satisfactory seed bed. A neighbour 'Butcher Robo' [2] had agreed to lend us his corn drill but could only spare it for one day. The only way we could have any chance of sowing twenty-five acres in a day was to start as soon as it was light in the morning; as it was the end of February there would be a good chance of frost on the ground enabling the operation to be started before the soil became a sticky mess, as it did later when the sun rose. Undaunted, we began in the dim first light only stopping for an hour for

48

milking and breakfast, allowing the heat of the sun to dry the slowly thawing surface of the soil. At 8.00 a.m. I went to work at Old Hall, Ganstead, and Geoff carried on drilling our barley back in the field. The variety was I remember, 'Julia', a variety that was particularly suited to our type of land. At noon I came home, grabbed a sandwich and a drink before taking over the sowing for half an hour while Geoff did the same when I went back to work. This process was repeated at tea-time and for the afternoon milking, thus the field was sown and the drill returned to 'Butcher Robo' before dark, all ready for his use the next day. Sixteen hour days were not unusual then when we seemed to have both the energy and the ambition to enjoy it.

To prepare for an increase in the size of the dairy herd we under-sowed grass seed three weeks later among the growing barley crop so that after harvest and over the winter it would grow on and give us extra grazing in the spring, thereby supplementing the winter feed of hay, rolled oats and barley. The seed was applied by Geoff using a Fiddle Drill, a container carried on a shoulder strap in front of the operator that has a spinning disc on to which the seed drops. The disk is rotated back and forth by a leather cord wound round the spindle and attached to a bow, much like playing a violin but with one stroke to each pace across the field and gives a spread of about four yards. To obtain an even coverage you walk the field at two yard intervals – in a twenty-five acre field you can imagine how many miles Geoff and I walked that day. The four acre field situated half a mile away down the lane was planted with rows of kale to become the cows' extra winter forage crop.

Of course Dad supplied us with the grass seed. It was one of the mixtures which he sold as the Manager of seed merchants M. M. Hirchfield & Co. in Hull. The names of the different types of grass and clover in the mixture, 'New Zealand Wild White Clover', 'Timothy', 'Meadow Fescue' or 'Italian Ryegrass' and 'Birdsfoot Trefoil' conjure up memories of when I was a small boy sitting in the company's High Street office where one window overlooked the River Hull with the barges going to-and-fro, while a large bay window to the side of the room looked out on to the garden of Wilberforce House, the former home of William Wilberforce, leader of the successful movement to abolish the slave trade. In front of the window stood a large oak table with trays of seed under glass, 100 seeds in each to test the germination rate. After a few days the seeds that had sprouted (germinated) were counted and the result confirmed or denied the specified germination rate of the sample. Dad's desk was raised on a plinth in the other window to gain the most benefit from daylight and his chair was made with extra-long legs to make it the same height.

The cows and my wages continued to provide some regular income for us, and applications of fertiliser to both grass and corn led to a reasonable harvest. There was plenty of work for Geoff to either hand hoe the kale or gradually improve the buildings, some of which had been used to house pigs in the past. Coincidently Mr Elliott had rather speculatively bought an imported Danish Landrace Boar and knowing we would need a boar to serve our five pigs when they had had their litters he 'persuaded' Geoff to buy it from him. Landrace were thought to be the breed of the future as they were longer in the body and leaner than the traditional Yorkshire Large White, producing a carcase with more rashers of leaner meat. The Danes had been rather clever by using Yorkshire Large Whites as a base but selecting offspring for extra length to eventually produce the Landrace pig.

One of our sows began to give us cause for concern by going off its food. We immediately called the vet, Richard (Dick) Joblin, at a time when most vets considered pigs to be not worth the effort, indeed many in the profession would not even turn out to see a pig, with 'Knock it on the head' being the most likely advice. The veterinary practice of Joblin and Oldham however was very far-sighted in its approach for Holderness was soon to become the foremost pig keeping region in the country with the result that they then became the leading veterinary specialists in the field. Mr Joblin (we were young and too polite to call him Dick) diagnosed very acute gastro-enteritis, and in his opinion it would be a miracle if she survived the week but it was worth trying to save her. Conscious that to us that she represented one fifth of our herd, we tried to get her to drink some milk with little success at first but gradually in increasing amounts, though for many days we opened the pen each morning wondering if she would be alive or dead. Lots of 'tender loving care' and the skill of a very good vet saved the day and the sow went on with the rest to provide the nucleus of a herd of longer, leaner pigs. Nonetheless, it was to be a good few years before we were able to keep pigs on a much larger scale.

With the cows in the yard for the winter, chopping thick stalks of kale with a billhook to load on to a trailer by hand was a cold wet but necessary task performed every morning come rain, snow or shine, an inevitability that resulted in painful cracked and sore hands. The particularly wet winter made getting the loaded tractor and trailer out of the distant, four acre field a work of art. Our only access to the field being two hundred yards down a narrow mud track that was soon reduced to two axle-deep wheel tracks filled with rain water. The only way to do it was to drive flat out in second gear with water coming up over the tractor foot rests and spraying up from the rear wheels carving a path through the mud to reach the tarmac road.

Eventually winter gave way to spring and as the fields dried out, the grass began to grow in response to our early application of fertiliser. The cows sniffing the air, sensed that turning out time was near and became very restless, seeking an opportunity to escape the confines of the yard, that was now so full of accumulated bedding that they could reach the barn roof with their heads. We were equally keen to benefit from the reduced workload that turning them out to graze would provide, for instead of cutting and carting freezing wet kale every day, the much more pleasant job of simply moving an electric fence a few yards twice a day would provide them with nice fresh grass, to which they would hopefully show their appreciation by increasing their milk output substantially. Spring was also a good time to consider buying more cows or more precisely some in-calf heifers. [3]

Our original cows had by now been artificially inseminated by the 'A.I. Man', [4] jokingly referred to as 'the bull with a bowler hat'. We had chosen a Friesian bull with the impressive name of 'Ironsides Texan', whom we hoped would provide us with some heifers to be registered under our herd name prefix of 'Taybro'. The first of these was eventually born and christened 'Taybro Topper'.

Topper being our first calf became a bit of a pet and would come over to us for a stroke usually nudging her head to be patted. This was fine when she was small but became more of a problem as she grew from a calf into a heifer and then a fully grown cow for nudges, then, especially if you were up against a wall, were less welcome.

Inevitably temperaments of cows vary considerably. One of ours could, if startled, virtually climb up the milking parlour wall, another was a notorious kicker when being milked. We soon learned the knack of pushing your head as hard as you could between the offending animal's ribcage and back leg so that it could only kick backwards not forwards as you applied the milking machine. During this process an uninitiated observer would be startled to see what appeared to be a headless man milking a cow.

In July 1958, and at the ripe old age of 21, I set off with Geoff to Staxton near Scarborough to collect my birthday present – an ex-U.S. Army, Willys Jeep, with its bonnet emblazoned with a large white star. As it was not taxed to be driven on the road we decided to tow it behind our Hillman Husky, unfortunately within half a mile we had to climb the 1:4 Staxton Hill. This task was achieved by starting the jeep engine and 'assisting' the poor little Husky whilst it was still being technically on-tow. I have no idea if that was legally correct but fortunately it was never put to the test – in other words we got away with it.

Trying to prove the jeep could drive across a ditch.

My Jeep was to fulfil many roles over the years such as towing harrows in the fields. As it consumed petrol at the rate of 10 to 12 miles per gallon, we developed the procedure of running it for ten minutes each morning on petrol until the engine was hot, then filling the fuel tank with very much cheaper paraffin, on which it could run all day. This was quite legal providing it was not driven on the public highway. Alternatively, it became a unique and popular mode of transport to Saturday night dances in Hull, although Arthur, the doorman at the New York Hotel in the city, cringed every time we parked on the road directly outside the entrance, lowering the tone of the place significantly. In fact he used to try and arrange it so that anyone with a more appropriate vehicle filled this prime parking place before we arrived.

Summertime Saturday nights often included a trip to the Candlelight Club on Scarborough's Bland's Cliff, a very steep cobble-stoned street that the jeep could take in its stride, especially in four-wheel drive mode. I naively hoped that its uniqueness would give me an advantage when chatting up the girls of the 'Television Toppers' dance troupe, who were at the time appearing on the *Black And White Minstrels Show* [5] at the Futurist Theatre next door. They often came into the Club after the evening's performance. Regrettably they will never know what they missed, and neither would I.

An unfortunately too successful situation with the jeep developed one night in Hull, beginning at the New York Hotel Christmas Eve Dance, when a few friends asked for a lift home in the jeep, that I had parked at Queen's Gardens with the intention of visiting the City Hall for the last half hour of the celebrations. Again there were people wanting transport home. By that time I had forgotten just how many I had said 'Yes' to so was completely unprepared for the crowd I found assembled around the jeep. Apparently, I had offered them all a lift and as we were in party mood I managed to pile twelve on board. As we began to reverse out a policeman appeared, holding up his hand to stop the pile of merry-makers who were doing a creditable impression of a motor cycle acrobatic display team but on four wheels instead of two. The Constable asked Mike, who was sitting in the right-hand side front seat, if he had full control of the vehicle, to which Mike replied, pointing to me, 'No but he has.' Mercifully nobody laughed when the Officer realised that the jeep was left hand drive. Ignoring the two people sitting facing backwards on the bonnet and folded down windscreen, and others piled precariously in the back, he slowly with the measured pace policemen adopt in such circumstances, circled the jeep before repeating the question to me. Amazingly accepting that I was 'in control' he waved us out of the car park and on our merry way.

As a rumoured party at somebody's house never materialized (must have been the product of a Chinese whisper), my passengers were dropped off gradually at their respective homes. The evening's brush with the law didn't end there however, when with only Mike and I left to make our way home, we were overtaken by a police car on Holderness Road and signalled to stop. Once again the measured circling of the jeep culminated in the worrying withdrawal of a police notebook for the listing of items of concern:

1. Front Number Plate obscured by mud.
2. Rear Number Plate obscured by mud.
3. Missing rear view mirror (Knocked onto the floor earlier).
4. In-appropriate side lights (Dessert army, slit type).
5. Driving license not signed.
6. Tax Disk not displayed (Same fate as the rear view mirror).
7. Inefficient Handbrake.

This latter problem came to light when, with the brake fully applied, the officer was able to push us down the road with one hand.

Seeing the address on my driving license he said, 'Oh! So you're a farmer are you?' This apparently changed the whole situation and for the second time that night I was waved on my way, apparently without a criminal record or an endorsement on my license. An explanation of my lucky escape came when weeks later I read a report in the local paper of a policeman being reprimanded for accepting 'favours' from some farmers in return for turning a blind eye to their various misdemeanors.

Harvest in my fourth year working at Old Hall Ganstead saw me day after day mowing with a scythe a nine acre field of badly flattened barley. As the field was alongside the main road in full view of passing buses and cars it must have resembled a scene from the Middle Ages and a far cry from the tractors and combine harvesters working on the land at the other side of the road. After weeks of back-breaking toil Richard Richardson, an Agricultural Contractor and our next door neighbour in Thirtleby, pulled up on the roadside and called over to tell me that he was so impressed with my dogged efforts that if I ever wanted to work for him I only had to ask. At the end of harvest that's exactly what I did, joining his muck spreading gang as a tractor driver loading the spreaders.

The winter months were spent moving from farm to farm loading and spreading, in rain sleet or snow, some days would be so cold that if you handled metal objects without wearing gloves your skin would immediately stick, frozen to whatever you had touched. One particular day it was so bitter that we built a small fire on the concrete block mounted on the back of my tractor, the purpose of the block was to add weight to the rear wheels to give extra grip but it also made a useful platform for the fire, the proximity of which at least kept my back warm. If I managed to load the spreaders very quickly there might even be time to turn round and warm my hands. This worked very well until the bottom of the ex-army greatcoat started to smoulder, a situation of which I was blissfully unaware, although I did wonder what my mates on the spreaders were laughing at. Eventually the smell of burning wool and increased heat on my back gave me a clue that something must be wrong with my on-board heating system. I leapt off the tractor with greatcoat well and truly alight ripping it off and jumping on it with my so-called 'mates' doubled up with laughter. It was to be many years before tractors were fitted with a safe and effective form of protection from the elements.

When spring came along and the livestock had been turned out to grass, our operations moved from the fields into the fold yards where the cattle had spent the winter. The spreaders were exchanged for tipping trailers but my job of filler driver stayed the same except for working in much more confined spaces, and I once calculated that I was achieving 3,000 gear changes per hour or more than one every second. With the favoured 'Little Grey Fergie' this caused it to occasionally engage two gears at the same time – forward and the reverse – stalling the engine immediately. The repair was effected by removing the oil filler cap on the gearbox, kept slightly loose on purpose, then inserting a long-bladed screwdriver into the works and flicking the reverse gear wheel back along its shaft. Bingo! The job was done and I was back to work in a couple of minutes.

Contracting in the summer began with the pea harvest. This involved fitting a cutting machine on to the back of the tractors that were then driven into the crop backwards so that cutters lifted and cut the crop depositing it in rows to one side or between the wheels of the tractor. The operator was provided with a seat fitted high up alongside the steering wheel facing backwards, steering with his right hand and operating the brakes and clutch through a complicated set of linkages and auxiliary pedals; this was akin to driving in reverse with your arms crossed, all the while looking in the mirror. Once a field was completed you changed back to the normal seat and driving position so as to drive forwards to the next job.

Occasionally a tip would be forthcoming from the farmer concerned, though the level of generosity varied considerably. One day the three of us had almost finished a particularly large and difficult field near Preston when the farmer came over in his new Land Rover, stopped alongside our foreman Dick Walker, who was repairing a broken cutter knife, and gave him a single sixpence suggesting that he 'Give the lads a drink.' While the farmer looked on Dick carefully placed the sixpenny piece on the anvil and with hammer and chisel cut the coin into three pieces. This apparently had no effect on the farmer who simply nodded, wound up his window and drove off.

1 Handing back part of the payment for livestock as thanks or in place of a guarantee.

2 Walter Robinson, who rented some land at Roe Hill nearby, had a butchers shop in Skirlaugh, hence his nickname.

3 A cow before it has had a calf.

4 The person who deals with the artificial insemination of cows.

5 *The Black and White Minstrel Show* was a British light entertainment show that ran on BBC television from 1958 to 1978 and was also a popular stage show.

7

Expansion

1962 was the year we decided that additional income on our limited acreage could be provided by rearing broiler chickens. A scheme was worked out for what would require purpose-built housing to accommodate 6,000 day-old chicks for rearing to ten weeks of age when they would be sold to the processing company. The funds for such a building would have to be borrowed from the bank who would naturally require the usual cash-flow projection showing how we intended to repay the loan.

Armed with cash-flow and specimen contracts from the processors, we set off for our appointment with the bank manager, intending to ask for sufficient funds to develop a unit holding 6,000 birds, however as we drove in to town we considered the possibility that the bank may suggest we reduce our plans to a more financially manageable 3,000, so we made the last minute decision to double our original figures and ask for finance for a 12,000 bird unit.

To our surprise the revised figure was accepted enabling us to sign contracts and begin work on the site in December. The foundations for the 40' x 250' foot building were hardly completed when in January, northerly winds accompanied by heavy snow completely blocked the lane with drifts up to six foot deep. The only way out was on foot. The digger working on our site could have been used to dig us out, but the driver had gone home with the keys and he could not be persuaded to brave the elements and return. Eventually we managed to force a way through or over the drifts and

Geoff sets out to walk a mile through six foot snow drifts to the main road.

across the fields with our tractor to collect some provisions, and rather more urgently take our full milk churns down to the main road at Coniston bringing back some much needed empty ones.

Digging our way out.

The main road into Hull was only just passable for the collection lorry but was blocked by the deep drifts beyond the village. On the third day we

this required the installation of a milk cartoning machine in our dairy and the installation of four vending machines in Hull; one outside a fish and chip shop on Hessle Road, one outside the Holderness sweet shop of ex-Hull city footballer Eddie Burbanks and one outside a newsagents also on Holderness Road. The fourth machine was placed in the canteen of William Jackson's bakery on Derringham Street.

The machines sold both milk and orange juice and with the exception of the ones outside sweet shops, Kit Kat chocolate bars, the taste of which was improved by being refrigerated that by happy coincidence further encouraged drink sales by making customers more thirsty. On hot summer nights it was often necessary to re-fill the machines at two hour intervals as in that short time they could each sell upwards of 200 cartons at 6d each. Emptying the coin boxes in the street at night, often surrounded by groups of youths was never a problem in the early days, but years later, vandalism made on-street sites uneconomical. Despite the fact that we had to pay a levy to the Milk Marketing Board for the privilege of selling our own milk, the business was very profitable, so much so that we used to weigh the bags of coins to take to the bank as there were too many to count by hand.

Eventually, it was decided to extend the service to provide hot drinks of tea, coffee, or chocolate and soups, and to move most of our operations indoors to factories and other places of work. Several machines were installed in the Ideal Standard foundry where we used Mini Vans for re-stocking as they were small enough to drive in and around machinery inside the buildings. Our policy was to place the refrigerated milk-vending machines in the hottest parts of the factory amongst the thirstiest workers. One good position was near the casting furnaces where the dust and heat made throats particularly dry.

An agreement to operate the Ross Group factory canteen in Hull provided the facility to produce additional hot meals packaged to sell via additional hot food vending machines that we had installed in other factories around Hull. Favourite vended hot meals included Fish and Chips, Roast Beef and Yorkshire Pudding, Shepherd's Pie, and a fantastic best seller, the specialty of our cook Mrs Wilson, her home-made Yorkshire Curd Cheesecake. On some sites spies from the factory floor would be sent early to the vending machine to check if it was on that day's menu, and there was always a rush to get in to the canteen before supplies ran out.

As more vending machines were installed in factories cousin Mike joined the business, bringing his electronics expertise to their maintenance. Mike had been an auto electrician with Globe and Simpson in Hull after doing his National Service in the R.E.M.E. (Royal Electrical and Mechanical Engineers) and continued to run the Maintenance Department of the vending company until his retirement.

The gradual move into workplace catering was a direct consequence of the increasing vandalism of the street sites, a common problem were attempts to break into the machines to steal cash or even just a carton of milk or a Kit Kat. It was becoming quite dangerous to open a machine for refilling at night because during the procedure the coin box was very vulnerable, though I found that the foot long angled steel device used to insert the cartons onto the refrigerated shelves would make a useful weapon should the need arise. My dog Duke in the passenger seat of the van was an added security measure especially if I encouraged him to bark when groups of youths came too near. Smashed display panels and even machines wrenched from their foundations became an increasingly frequent occurrence until eventually the reluctant decision was made to remove all the on-street machines.

Over the years the demands on our time of Falkingham and Taylor Vending Ltd, had clashed with the needs of the business of Taylor Brothers, Farmers. We realized that sharing the profits from vending with partner

Bruce, when it fell to us to do all the day to day work of running the business was not a fair reward for the effort involved, and detracted from us developing our farming enterprise. We relinquished our interest in the company in 1972, whilst continuing to supply carton-packaged milk until the company switched over to hot drinks and snacks.

Changes in farming as a result of the common agricultural policy of the EEC placed a new burden on the dairy industry and particularly on small dairy farmers like us. Thirty cows were not enough but 40 acres would not support many more. One possible answer was to 'zero graze', which is to grow grass more efficiently by applying large amounts of fertilizer, cutting fresh grass twice daily seven days a week, and carting it to more cows. In addition the recommendation was to feed extra concentrate cattle cake. Not surprisingly and with the benefit of hindsight this recommendation came from advisers to the cattle-feed manufacturers. In pursuit of this, we tried it for a year, at one point carrying a herd of nearly 50 cows on 40 acres.

The down-side of this system was that for 365 days a year grass had to be cut and carted morning and afternoon, cows needed bedding up every day using large amounts of bought-in straw, the bulk-feed lorry came almost as frequently as the milk tanker as did the bills from the feed mill. Every day for us was milking followed by feeding, followed by milking followed by more feeding. It must have been equally boring for the cows especially in spring when they could smell the newly cut grass but couldn't gallop off to eat it in the field. The only winners were the feed firms who increased their profits considerably. Needless to say we abandoned this system and reduced the herd back to a more manageable and conventional size.

The broiler chicken business proved very volatile as feed firms integrated with the processors and thereby controlled the profit margins to a large extent; our first crop had been the most profitable despite the day-old chicks arriving before the building had its roof on. The only dry areas on the floor were the twelve heated pads each with a 1,000 chicks penned on. Fortunately the roof was completed in time to allow them access to the whole building. Sixty automatic drinkers suspended from the roof supplied clean water to the birds and 100 tube-feeders filled every day by bucket from a hopper on a monorail system provided the feed.

At eight weeks the birds were ready for the processor and this required that they be caught and carried three or four in each hand and placed in crates on the processor's lorry. It took about three hours to load all 12,000 and for this we had a group of men we could call on for help. The team comprised policemen, farm workers, factory workers, in fact anybody who wanted to earn a bit of cash in hand and a chicken for the pot. The usual time to start catching was 3.00 a.m., to enable the first load to be at the factory for processing at 8.00 a.m. However, on one occasion a lad from the nearby village of Swine overslept and left us shorthanded. Geoff went to his house to knock him up by the time honored method of throwing gravel at the bedroom window. After two attempts the window opened showing a face and the unwelcome glint of shot-gun barrels illuminated by the moonlight, followed in quick succession by the shout, 'If you don't bugger off, I've got two up the spout of this thing.' Geoff quickly retreated, all the while shouting back: 'Are you coming broiler catching tonight'? I think maybe we managed with one short that night.

The worst situation for us occurred when three weeks after a crop had been sold and by which time we would normally have received payment from Kingston Poultry Services, we had a tip off on the Friday night that all was not well with their finances. On the Saturday morning when Geoff went to their offices in Beverley to get our cheque the door was locked and nobody answered the bell. The office of auctioneers Dee & Atkinson were in the same building so he went in and asked if they knew if anybody was in the office upstairs? They replied that they thought so and let him in by a connecting door. A very surprised and embarrassed manager of KPS reluctantly handed over the £3,000 cheque that we paid promptly into the bank as soon as it opened on Monday morning. Thankfully, it cleared before KPS went bust on the Wednesday. I think that if we had not got the money when we did they may well have taken us down with them.

The profitability of broiler production had begun to decline and an alternative that needed no new expenditure was to switch to rearing turkeys. Instead of 12,000 chickens the unit would house 6,000 turkeys. The main disadvantage with turkeys is that when they are born they have one main ambition, and that is to commit suicide by whatever means they can for they are completely stupid. A typical event for instance was when they were about a week old and I left a galvanized bucket on the floor whilst filling the feeders at the other end of the building. One chick had gone into the bucket and was pecking the end of it, and on hearing the ensuing noise every chick within earshot decided to pile into the bucket to investigate, with the result that in the time it took me to walk the hundred yards length of the building, five of the idiot birds had suffocated. You couldn't even swear at them as even a cough was enough to cause panic and pandemonium.

8
Building for the future

My social life then involved girlfriend Judy, leading to our subsequent engagement and this situation raised the future need for extra accommodation. Geoff had married Rita and for a time they had lived in a large caravan on the farm, subsequently buying a bungalow in Coniston. It was decided that we should try to get planning permission to build a bungalow in the orchard of Hill Farm. My education in architectural drawing at Hull Building College came in useful again and I drew up my own plans for a four bedroom chalet type bungalow.

Although I was fairly happy with the result a friend of Geoff's agreed to check them over for a small fee. Not wanting them to be rejected for a silly mistake I handed them over; he made a couple of very minor amendments and quoted a figure of several hundred pounds which he said was normal and based on the square footage of the finished building, in addition he would project manage the building work as it progressed. As all he had done was move a downstairs door nine inches and change an upstairs sliding door to an opening one, I offered him £40.00 cash for his work so far and that I would manage the project myself. It later transpired that the door he had moved would have had the stairs going right across the middle of it and the sliding door into the box room had been necessary because of the angle of the roof! I should have known if you want a job doing properly have confidence and do it yourself.

The first planning application to the Council was rejected on the grounds that this was a green belt area and no further residential development would be permitted unless essential for workers accommodation. One councillor, who had for a time lived in Thirtleby, suggested that were the council to allow this, Thirtleby was in danger of becoming a metropolis. Ignoring this outrageous claim, we tried to convince the council that it is essential for a livestock farm to have workers who are on site or nearby at all times. A further application was rejected because the planning officers were not happy with my intention to use 'green' tiles on the roof. I re-submitted the plans but on this occasion described the colour of the tiles as 'Lichen' and this was accepted even though lichen is in fact green so they were going to be exactly the same tiles.

Once more the plans went to the planning committee with a covering letter stressing the need for accommodation for myself on the farm, and finally they were at last accepted subject to what is known as an Agricultural Occupancy Clause. This states that the property can only be occupied by 'Someone Employed in Agriculture or the Dependents of Someone Employed in Agriculture'.

Although I was delighted we had succeeded, the condition threw up an unforeseen problem in that no building society would give me a mortgage, as they claimed the condition would mean that if I defaulted on the repayments they would not be able to sell the house to recover their loss. Up against this stumbling block, I contacted the council planning department again, pointing out that they had created an impossible situation by imposing the restrictive Agricultural Condition. They suggested I should apply for a council mortgage that could be granted in exceptional circumstances. I was not aware that such a thing existed and immediately applied for a loan of £3,500, making it clear that it was the council's own rules and regulations that had created the need for this.

With the mortgage secured I was able to start preparing the site, which in the past had been the orchard but was now just a few very old trees and badly overgrown with nettles. The foundations were dug out and the first of many loads of ready-mixed concrete laid in them. Two bricklayers and a labourer had answered my advertisement in the local paper and we agreed a price of £300.00 cash for the job. I had estimated it would take 10,000 bricks and 2,000 concrete blocks. At the end we had six blocks and 200 bricks left over and they proved just enough to build a wall on the drive. The contractors who tiled the roof were even more accurate in their estimating, having only one tile left over. The bricklaying gang only worked at weekends but completed their part of the build in seven weeks or just 14 days actual work.

As mentioned, the site had been an old orchard and was very overgrown with brambles and nettles almost waist high but scything and clearing the area enabled us to peg out the outline of the house. Digging out the foundations by hand ready for concreting made the rooms look very small, but a feature of house building is that it seems to either expand or contract several times during construction. The laying of six tons of ready-mix concrete was made much easier when the driver of the mixer lorry took one look at the dry roadside ditch, engaged its' six wheel drive and drove straight across so that he could discharge the concrete directly into position right around the site. All that was left for us to do was a final leveling, and what could have been a back-breaking job of barrowing and shoveling was done in less than an hour.

Mr Myers, the building inspector, approved the foundations enabling the brickies to build up to damp-course level the following weekend. We then filled the internal floor area with hardcore and compacted sand covered with a thick layer of polythene damp-proofing material topped off with four inches of screeded concrete. In spite of the best efforts of our now familiar ready-mix driver this was as back-breaking as his previous visit had been easy. Another weekend and our gang of brickies built the external walls up to the height where they would need scaffolding before they could continue, requiring that I develop a new skill as a scaffold erector. This proved to be much like Meccano for big boys and all was made ready for their next weekend visit. In this fashion, doing as much as I could of the less skilled work and making sure that everything was on site when needed by the professionals, the building took shape very quickly indeed.

Our house 'Seasons' as viewed from the back garden.

Regrettably, before the house was completed, Judy realized a future life as a farmer's wife was not for her, and we parted to remain good friends. I pressed on in my spare time installing the plumbing and central heating system. One day as I was fitting the kitchen cupboards a complete stranger came in wanting to know if I would take an offer for the house? I told him it was not for sale. He said he had heard in the pub that I had built it intending to get married and as this had fallen through might want to sell. Typical small village gossip, everybody knows your business better than you know it yourself. He did not want to take no for an answer and offered me £16,000 as it stood; this when it had cost me less than £3,000 at that stage, convinced me I had made a good investment. I told him I wouldn't sell it, not even for £20,000, knowing that this would get back to the village gossips. Thirty years later it was to be valued at almost £300,000.

9

A new beginning

Two years later my very good friend of many years, Mike Hall, persuaded me to go on a blind date to meet two girls at the pub in Lund near Beverley. One was a friend of his called Jane Crabtree, to whom we quickly gave the nickname 'Lobsterbush', and the other her friend Angela, who lived in a cottage with her baby daughter Sally. Angela was separated from husband Bob and awaiting completion of their divorce. Games of dominoes started the evening off very well with the girls wining most of them, before returning to Angela's cottage for supper where Mike and I offered to fry the sausages we had spied in the tiny kitchen. Slightly merry on a mixture of a little lager and a lot of laughter we thought we might impress the girls with our cooking skills so decided to add a splash of wine to the sizzling sausages. This was a very bad move as the resulting conflagration spattered fat all over us and worst still the walls and ceiling of the little kitchen.

I immediately offered to redecorate the kitchen and luckily the offer was accepted – I seem to remember the sausages tasted fine too. The return visit provided an opportunity to meet Angela again and though I had previously been conscripted into taking somebody else in a group of friends to the Hunt Ball, persuaded Jane and Angela to come along with Mike. It proved to be quite a difficult evening, as I was torn between not offending Sue, my partner for the Ball, whilst wanting to be with Angela, it did however convince me who I would rather be with if there was to be a next time.

After a while Angela's divorce came through and we were seeing each other in the little cottage most evenings and at the weekends. On one occasion we both fell asleep in front of the sitting room fire and on another a warm place elsewhere in the cottage, not waking until 5.00 a.m. I arrived home that morning just in time to pass Dad coming down the stairs. He never asked where I had been and I hastily changed into my work clothes ready for milking as if nothing had happened. All the coming and going to see Angela at the cottage was very inconvenient for us, so I suggested that she and Sally move into the now fully completed 'Seasons'. Whilst working in the house I had always felt it had a peaceful and warm atmosphere, and interestingly though Sally was now two years old, she had never slept through the night at the cottage. On the first night at 'Seasons' she slept soundly through until the morning and continued to do so almost every night from then on.

On 16 March 1974, Angela and I were married at the Beverley Registry Office. 'Seasons' immediately became more than a house, it was now our family home. A few weeks before the wedding we had taken Sally with us to Hull to buy a wedding ring and while we were choosing one from a selection of rings in the jewellers, Sally promptly informed the shop assistant that Mummy, Daddy John and her were going to get married. We had told her earlier that we were all getting married together to make a new family, so Mummy would need a ring and Sally would need a ring in the form of a silver bracelet. Though slightly taken aback by Sally's bold revelation the assistant entered fully into the spirit of the occasion as both ring and bracelet were selected. As we had been married as a family, all three of us went on honeymoon together stopping the night at the Collingwood Arms Hotel in Cornhill on Tweed, before moving on to stay at the Coylumbridge Hotel near Aviemore.

On 18 December 1974, our second daughter Helen was born, a lovely little sister for Sally. A few days after she was born I came down from the pigs, noticing a small pair of shoes on the doorstep. As they were very small indeed I thought they might belong to one of Sally's friends, but for some reason that even now I cannot explain, jokingly shouted, 'Look out Angie, Swine vicar's here.' Before she could answer I was through the door, joining Angela and the vicar of Swine in person in the kitchen. Our previous encounter with him had not left us with much appetite for social chit-chat and he eventually got the message and left.

When he had gone Angela told me that on seeing baby Helen in the Moses basket he had asked when she had been born, all the while openly adding up the months since our wedding on his fingers. He must have been disappointed when he exceeded the nine month barrier by a full two days.

Our lack of bonhomie towards him, which derived from our first contact with him eighteen months prior when we had approached him with a request to be married in Swine Church. At that meeting he had told us that because Angela was divorced, '… his Bishop and the Church of England would not allow it.' Then, without further explanation or apology, he suddenly left his chair and knelt down, suggesting that we pray for Angela, as if she needed forgiveness! He was still on his knees praying fervently as we walked out and left him to it.

So after this fruitless visit and at the recommendation of our friend Jill Binns, we made an appointment to see the vicar of the nearby Parish of Sproatley. The Reverend Weinstock was an ex-Navy man who had converted from the Jewish faith to be ordained into the Church of England and who although bound by the same rules and regulations as the vicar of Swine, was much more understanding of our situation. He genuinely regretted he could not marry us until the rules were changed, suggesting instead that we could have a civil wedding followed by a service of blessing in his church, though strictly speaking we did not live in his parish.

He was to my mind a true Christian and very down to earth for it was his opinion that most people wanted a church wedding primarily because it was traditional, posh and showy – also the photos would look better in the album than a wedding at the local registry office. He said he had first-hand experience of this with his own family wedding due shortly. From that day on we considered Sproatley to be our local church.

10
Family life

We now had two wonderful daughters, Sally Jane and Helen Catherine, and sixteen months later on St George's Day, 23 April 1976, a baby brother, Jonathan David or as he came to be known, 'Jona', was born.

My memories of this time are of children's ponies, pet lambs and Labradors, and skiing holidays though they came later, in fact four years later because for four years we had no holiday away from the farm at all. Angela's memories are probably of washing, cooking, and being a taxi service for whoever needed running somewhere of other but I hope that like me, the vast majority of her memories of those days are of very happy times.

Helen, Jonathan, and Sally.

One game that Sally used to play required the assistance of Simba our golden Labrador, when she would sit on an old piece of carpet and he would pull her around the garden looking like the Queen of Sheba on a magic carpet ride. Or she would be sitting on the swing suspended from the branch of a large apple tree and when Simba saw her he would dash up and grab hold in his teeth the rope that was hanging under the seat, turning her round and round several times before letting go, and all the while she spun faster and faster as the swing un-twisted itself. Helen would probably be pushing Jona' in a little trolley that normally held wooden alphabet blocks, or they would be playing in the sandpit contained in a huge tractor back tyre, painted blue so that the black rubber didn't mark their clothes.

All the children were very loving to us both though I remember Helen was one for almost constant cuddles with Dad, and when we were visiting people she would be almost sitting on my knee. I remember this particularly because one day Angela pointed out she was getting too old as she was probably about nine or ten at the time. Even now I tell them that they are never too old for hugs and hugs are a fine compromise.

As they all got older ponies became the big attraction so a piece of field had to be fenced off and a stable constructed. They were used to animals of all kinds. On one occasion Sally came into the piggery where a sow was due to farrow (to give birth) during the night. All our pigs were Large Whites crossed with Landrace, but Sally told the sow she wanted a 'spotty' pig the next day. I tried to explain that the baby pigs would be all-white and we had never had any 'spotty' pigs. The next morning to my surprise there were 10 white piglets and two black-spotted ones in the pen, an event I recounted as a note of warning to her husband Adam in my speech at her wedding many years later.

Christmas Day on the farm had its own routine beginning with the children opening the presents that Father Christmas had left in their stockings at the end of the bed. Meanwhile, I went out to feed the animals and milk the cows with Geoff; this would usually take until about 11.00 a.m. when we would all sit round and Jona' and the girls would distribute the presents that were piled under the Christmas tree in the corner of the lounge, and we would try to keep pace with them by writing down which present was for whom and from whom. Angela was very good at instilling into the children that you must always write thank you letters after Christmas, a practice which much to my admiration they have passed on to their own children to this day.

One very memorable Christmas involved very clandestine arrangements to provide Jona' with his present. He would, I think, have been about eight or nine years old and frequently came to the cattle market with me when we had pigs to sell, and would often jump into the aisles and help us move sheep into various pens prior to being sold; most of the men didn't mind for they always encouraged farmer's sons who showed an interest in livestock. He had often told me that he would like his own sheep on the farm, so one day I mentioned this to Peter Caley, a well-known local farmer who had often seen Jona' helping to pen his sheep. 'Well then', Peter said, 'we must encourage this, come and see me a couple of days before and we will find him an in-lamb ewe for Christmas.'

How to keep this a secret from Jona' was the main problem. The afternoon of Christmas Eve, I took a trailer behind my car and bought a ewe from Peter's farm near Beverley. It had plenty of room and food and water in the trailer, so I was able to hide it for while at our piggery. Just after midnight, I managed to get the sheep into the garage and luckily the animal did not make a sound as I reversed past Jona's bedroom window dropping the trailer off and shutting the garage door. Mission accomplished so far, with just three hours in bed and up early at 4.00 a.m. to let the sheep quietly into the garden. I returned to bed, as though nothing had happened, just in time before excited voices indicated that Christmas stockings were being plundered for presents. However, so busy was everyone with the presents that Father Christmas had brought, nobody, least of all Jona', looked out of the window. In desperation, as the sheep started to eat the flowers in the border, I said to Jona', 'Look! There is a loose reindeer in the garden!' for that was all I could think of at the time. Jona' shot over to the window and shouted, 'No Dad, it's a sheep! Oh, thank you Father Christmas, it is my bestest present ever!'

A few weeks later the ewe produced twin lambs one of which was to be called Woolmer, but for the life of me I can't remember the name of the other.

Eventually, as is the case in farming, they grew bigger and the time came when they had to go to the butcher. We usually brought one back butchered ready for the deep freeze though at first the children did not want the same ones back, so we agreed to get another one from the butcher instead. However, after some thought, Jona' wanted to be a real farmer so said he didn't mind if we had Woolmer back. We told him it would be better

Woolmer. Need I say more?

not to say anything to the girls about his change of mind. The following Sunday Angela had cooked lunch and told Jona' to shout to the girls to tell them dinner was ready. As little brothers tend to do on these occasions he went to the door and shouted at the top of his voice, 'Come on girls, Woolmer's on the Table!'

We all sat down to our delicious lamb, two veg, and roast potatoes, noticing that Jona', who up to that point had been one tough little boy, was now staring at his food, knife and fork in hand, but with a tear running down both cheeks. Yet, he ate it all, but not long after this episode the girls began to think that vegetarianism was an attractive option.

Ponies began to make an appearance on the farm when I bought a little grey pony called Holly (yes, I know Holly is not a boy's name but Holly it was) who was what is known as 'bomb proof', that is he would never attempt to unseat a rider although he could be stubborn at times. When we bought him he was quite old and though we sold him eventually, Helen visited him at his last home near Lockington in East Yorkshire many years later and by then he must have reached at least 30 years of age.

Bomb proof Holly.

Angela had a horse named Captain who once, when we had temporarily stabled him on a friend's farm two miles away, decided to join in with the Holderness Hunt when it was out for a day's foxhunting by jumping over an eight foot wide cattle grid and racing along the lane, through two villages, before crossing the busy Hull to Bridlington main road, miraculously avoiding all the traffic in the process while several huntsmen galloped alongside in hot pursuit hoping to stop him. They only just caught up with him as he jumped the gate into his own field back at home.

Angela's 'homing' horse, Captain.

Helen on Tanzy.

Sally was a member of the local Young Farmers Club and entered a competition to rear a calf to sell at the auction market with the winner being the person whose calf made the most money. The day of the sale arrived and I joined in the bidding trying to run the price up to help Sally get the best she could. I think the auctioneer realized what I was doing so he began taking bids 'off the wall' – in other words imaginary bids – and I was actually bidding against myself, the outcome being that I bought what was almost a little bullock that came back home with us.

Sally and her calf in the auction ring.

Jona' animal training.

**Little Boy Blue and Sally's bullock.
Surely this is what life is all about?**

Family life was as near as perfect as it could be, with three lovely children and a wife who enjoyed the countryside every bit as much as I did. Although financially life was at times 'very tight' and there was a period of four years when we couldn't afford and so didn't have a holiday at all. Even the years when were able to take some time off the children began to believe that it always rained at the seaside, steming from the fact that during harvest or haymaking and if it was a rainy day I would say, 'Come on, we can't work today, it's too wet, so let's all go to the beach.'

As any farmer will tell you agricultural life has its lean and its fat years, although he is more likely to say, 'Lean and not quite so lean years.' During some of the lean ones we actually qualified for family income support but we stuck at it and got through in the end. Looking back some of our married friends seemed to have enough money yet were not any happier than we were as they were frequently arguing or having blazing rows, on occasions seemingly on the brink of breaking up. They could never understand how Angela and I didn't have such arguments. I don't know the answer to that, just that I am forever grateful that it was so.

For me the family is everything and being able to provide for them is the most important part I can play. I had been brought up as a home-loving person, never straying far away from the nest. So I found it very hard to accept the opportunity, financially enabled by Angela's mother, for our children to go to private school in the hope that they would have a better chance to progress to university. Whilst I am eternally grateful now for the help and support she gave us over the years, I still worry about any homesickness they may have felt at the time. It must have been worthwhile however, because I am immensely proud of them and what they have since achieved.

11

Diversify to survive

Britain by joining the EEC had started the gradual decline of the British dairy industry and it became increasingly difficult to make a living from such a small farm and a herd of 40 or so cows. The talk was of 'butter mountains', 'wine lakes' and too much milk, so as an encouragement small dairy farmers were offered payment to leave milk production altogether. Our alternative would be to plough up all the grasses and grow cereals. In 1976 arrangements were made for the sale of the dairy herd and all associated milking equipment. A sale ring was set up in the covered yard with the auctioneer's rostrum on our flat bale trailer. The auctioneer asked us to fix up a powerful spotlight behind him shining directly into the eyes of the bidders, the reason for this was that he wanted to be able to see them better than they could see him. It seemed to work very well as each animal was walked through the ring to brisk bidding from the flood-lit buyers. At the end of the day only the bulk tank and an eerily empty milking parlour remained to be washed down for the last time.

We calculated that the ploughed out grasses should yield a good crop of winter wheat the following year but in the meantime we would have to manage without the monthly milk cheque. We knew that two families could not make a living without some intensive livestock and fattening pigs could provide the answer. It was decided to build what are known as solari type rearing pens, these are simply open-fronted low-roofed pens built side by side each holding 60 pigs being weaned at six weeks of age until they were big enough to move into pens of 12 in a fattening house, where they stayed until they weighed about 200lbs or 90 kilos and eventually sold as bacon pigs. After visiting a farm recommended by our bank manager as a good example to follow, we drew up building plans and once more engaged the services of the bricklaying team who had built my bungalow. The eight solari pens were bedded up with deep straw, the full width doors on the front enabling easy access with tractor and front end loader for mucking out after each batch. A feed hopper and trough ran the full length of the rear of the pens providing feed ad-lib for the pigs, and automatic drinking bowls completed the pig's amenities.

The fattening unit contained 42 pens in two rows each side of a raised feeding passage, a dunging passage ran down each side of the building with gates dividing each pen, these could be closed to allow a scraper to push the ensuing slurry once a day into a pit at the far end. The raised central passage gave a good view of all the pigs, an important part of good animal husbandry. Feeding in the fattening house was by a liquid pipeline system. This comprised a mixer to mix dry meal with water which was pumped around a two inch pipeline with a tap at each pen feeding the mix down into a full width trough We found that opening the tap for a count of one second per pig in each pen twice a day delivered the correct amount of feed.

It was important to obtain good supplies of healthy weaned pigs preferably in multiples of 60 from as few sources as possible to minimize the chance of bringing disease onto the farm, and the best way to do this was to have an arrangement with a marketing group who could source pigs from the same 'store pig' producers on a regular basis. In this way the unit was gradually stocked with 480 weaners, eventually filling the fattening house and increasing the total to over 900 pigs.

Some of the output was sold to the Malton Bacon Factory, and to save on the cost of haulage we used our old Ford Transit van and a new Wards double axle livestock trailer fitted with two decks. We could get eight pigs into the back of the van and about 10 into the trailer. With this load aboard Geoff would make the journey to Malton, and although there was a plywood partition to prevent the pigs joining Geoff in the front, it was not entirely 'pong' proof and even with the windows open it got quite hot and smelly in the front.

We also used this van to collect weaners from Steve Willerton, who farmed near Pickering. Late one evening, just before Christmas, I had collected 60 weaners from Steve and noticed several police cars stationed at crossroads along the route. Thinking they were possibly on the lookout for poultry thieves at that time of the year, I drove past a couple of them without incident until one came up behind me in Wetwang village, following and flagging me down in Tibthorpe. I think the steam issuing from the van windows had aroused his suspicions so to lighten the load and before he could say anything I said, 'It's OK officer I haven't any chickens just pigs. 'It's pigs we are looking for' he said, 'where did you get them?' I gave him Steve's address and my details, which, as it was the middle of the night didn't fully convince him. He must have passed the information on ahead because I was shadowed by other patrol cars at intervals all the way back to Thirtleby.

Using our home-grown wheat and barley for feed was the next development and required the purchase of a secondhand hammer mill that had been used in Bradshaw's Flour Mill at Driffield. It had a capacity far in excess of anything we might need and is the reason why it was cheap, and it also came with enough spares to last a lifetime at the rate we would be using it. Four old telegraph poles, some timber and corrugated iron were used to construct a large barn to house the mill and a feed mixing plant bought new from our very good friend Pat Bailey at Horstine Farmery Ltd. Pat had worked for the same firm as it passed via takeovers by several different owners, from leaving school to his retirement. With experience we began to improve the feed and as a result the performance of the pigs too.

I had become interested in computers and bought a Commodore 65 which operated in 'Basic' language, the mathematical logic of which I found extremely interesting. Purchasing a book entitled *Teach Yourself Basic* I spent hours writing simple small programs to run on the computer. It then occurred to me that I might be able to write a program that could work out all the calculations to find the best and most cost-effective ration for our pigs. The eventual result was line after line of programming that when printed out ran to dozens of pages of text. All we had to do was enter the current price of the available ingredients and the levels of protein, fibre, oil, and lysine etc., which we required in the end result. The program contained the standard percentages of protein, fibre, oil and lysine for each ingredient, and so very quickly calculated the most cost-effective mix. So began my interest in the use of computers in agriculture.

Although the feeding of the pigs was fairly well organized the purchase of suitable weaners from as few sources as possible on a regular basis was proving increasingly difficult. This coincided with a decline in the profit from turkeys and convinced us it would be better to cease turkey production and convert the turkey shed into a pig breeding unit to produce our own weaners. We purchased an electric welder and a huge quantity of secondhand galvanized steel tube, and with these we taught ourselves the almost black art of welding. We began by constructing a jig and on it mounted a Black and Decker circular saw with a plentiful supply of abrasive metal cutting disks. The tube was cut to the required lengths to make 200 individual sow stalls. The first few attempts at welding would have attracted extremely rude comments from any self-respecting blacksmith. The solution at first was to knock our welds apart with a sledge hammer and try again, the fact that you could do this was proof that they were rubbish. After a while we got much more proficient until they became impossible to knock apart and that's when we knew we were good enough welders to go into production. Changes to the concrete floor of the old broiler building were necessary to provide a dry lying area and dung channels while at the same time installing the now welded steel pen dividers and individual glazed feeding troughs providing dry-sow accommodation for up to 200 sows. Eight boar serving pens with five foot high concrete block walls were built halfway down the building. With the remaining space split into two rooms, each with 24 farrowing crates in four rows of six pens, each pen fitted with an infra-red heat lamp.

More steel tube and more cutting and welding produced 48 farrowing crates, the first 24 of which Angela carefully and laboriously painted by hand despite being very pregnant at the time. This entailed her crawling on hands and knees, baby bulge and all, inside each crate. When it came to painting the remaining 24, much to Angela's totally justified disgust, we decided that we would paint them with a mechanical spray gun. My excuses for doing it this way was not helped when some of the silver spray mist was blown onto the bungalow windows and even worse on to Angela's car.

Stocking of the new unit was achieved by selecting and retaining the best performing gilts from the fattening house, moving them into the now completed boar pens to be served by boars bought from JSR farms. The pregnant gilts were duly housed in the stalls until a few days before they were due to farrow in the first of the beautifully painted crates.

By this method we gradually stocked the breeding side and eventually as our own little pigs were born we were able to gradually reduce the numbers needed to be bought in, yet, with almost the last batch disaster struck on discovering that they had Rhinitis, a debilitating deformation of the nostrils adversely affecting breathing. The supplier of the pigs claimed he had not seen any signs of this in his herd and as it was not always apparent until the little pigs got older. It was a severe blow to us as it compromised the minimal disease status we were aiming for by being self-contained.

Gradually and perhaps inevitably the Rhinitis spread to affect at first only the occasional pig in our herd but over time more and more began to suffer as they became infected. Once the disease is established the only answer is complete de-stocking of the whole unit, followed by a thorough treatment with a powerful disinfectant. This would entail a period when we would have nothing to sell, resulting in no income and severe cash flow problems. One answer would be to buy a ready-made replacement herd with sows at various stages of pregnancy, ready to move in once our buildings had had an important few weeks empty of livestock, this being a crucial part of the disinfecting regime.

An ideal situation arose when JSR farms, suppliers of our original boars, decided to clear out one of their herds prior to re-stocking with a new genetic line. The JSR herd was in perfect health and full production, so we negotiated to buy them at a very competitive price as they needed to move them all as one lot in three months' time. This was exactly what we wanted, so a date was agreed that we could meet if we started our de-stocking immediately; this then gave us nine weeks to de-stock and three weeks disinfected and stood empty. Seven weeks later there was an outbreak of Swine Vesicular Disease ten miles away. Consequently a Ministry ban on all movement of pigs was put in place. We still had the last few pigs on the farm that should have been moved in a weeks' time so as to begin the three week empty period before the arrival of the new herd. The movement order was not lifted for three weeks giving us only one week fully disinfected and empty.

To save time and as each building became free, we started to clean them out and as an extra precaution we pressure-washed and disinfected every nook and cranny, mixed the disinfectant with white emulsion paint and sprayed everything from top to bottom. By doing this we knew that if it was white it must have been disinfected and so should be both sterile and safe. Eventually the new herd of in pig sows started to arrive from JSR Farms with the ones nearest to farrowing (giving birth) the first to be delivered, then those with a week or two to go and most recently served, next came the ones ready to be put to the boars, and a final load contained weaned pigs at various stages of growth. They all settled in quite well but only time would tell if the enforced hold up to our de-stocking program and hence the severely restricted cleaning time had compromised our plans.

A very serious effect on profitability at this time was the declining price of finished pigs at the markets set against rapidly rising cereal prices. Although some of our feed was provided by the wheat and barley we grew ourselves, the truth was that the cereals we grew could have been sold straight off the combine at a profit. Instead they were fed to our pigs, eventually to be taken to market and sold for whatever the buyers decided to pay on the day, often representing a loss. Animal health rules meant that pigs sold at a 'fat-stock' market (pigs sold for killing) could not be returned to a farm and must go directly to an abattoir for slaughter. The buyers therefore had total control of the price, the only competition being among themselves, they hardly ever 'fell out', but if they did then a more realistic price ensued. I have heard of farmers starting a whispering campaign to try and start an argument between two buyers in order to 'jack the prices up a bit'.

In 1995 it was this un-business-like way of selling pigs that led me to consider breaking away from a system that encouraged farmers to spend weeks of their time and lots of their money, or more likely their bank's money, producing something for which they then simply took whatever price they were offered without any option to say no. Any other product would be taken back if it could not be sold at a profit. Whilst pigs could not stay on the farm indefinitely there should be a system which gives adequate time to seek the best price before they are finally sent to an abattoir for slaughter.

Sadly in 1987 our Mum, who lived in the farm house died suddenly. Geoff and I had both built our own houses on the farm, thus the farm house would now be empty and none of our children were at an age to put it to good use. We realized that 40 acres, even if it was farmed intensively, could never support two growing families. I wanted to try and keep the farm if possible as Jona', though only 12-years old, was showing signs of wanting to become a farmer whereas Geoff and Rita's children, Debra and Phillip, sought their futures elsewhere.

In the spring of 1988 it was decided that if I could raise the funds to buy Geoff's share of the farm I would continue, in the hope that Jona' would take up farming when he got older. To do this, we had to sell the old farmhouse and eight acres of land, and with additional financial help from Angela's Mum, we reached a mutually satisfactory agreement. Within a week Geoff was approached by the local golf club who were expanding from a nine-hole course to eighteen. He became their head groundsman as his farming experience would be an invaluable asset to them.

Of course I needed to consider other means of increasing our income and this led me to explore further my ideas about the use of computers in agriculture. In the days when I wrote the program to create the most cost-efficient feed rations for our pigs there had been systems called Compulink and CompuServe that with the aid of a Modem (Modulator/Demodulator) changed key strokes on a computer into sounds (Modulated), which could be transmitted down a telephone line to be changed back (Demodulated) to appear as the letters or numbers or even blocks of colour on a computer screen at the other end of the line. The problems of marketing pigs through traditional livestock auctions set me thinking about the possibility of creating an auction where the pigs would not leave the farm until they had been sold for a price acceptable to the producer.

The answer was to become Tabrotec my online computer based auction, a concept which now in 2013 is quite normal but back then in 1987 was just my pipe dream.

12

Tabrotec is born

My experience with the computer and the development of 'Prestel' (a forerunner of the internet) encouraged me to give serious consideration to the possibility of running live auctions on computers, whereby farmers could offer their pigs with a reserve price to several buyers at abattoirs all over the country, and buyers could bid independently, with the highest bidder over the reserve being successful. Pigs who did not reach the reserve would remain on the seller's farm and unlike those sold in a traditional livestock market would not be committed by law for slaughter at any price that was offered on the day.

With Prestel, screen 'refresh' times were quite slow, simply because of the amount of text on each page. What I envisaged would only require a price in pence per kilo to be updated, so at the most three characters would be involved and refresh would be almost instantaneous. Any other information on the screen would only change when the next 'lot' was displayed.

Reading in the paper that the giant electrical company GEC had a 'cash mountain', which it needed to invest, but in addition had a Prestel telecommunications department, I decided to go straight to the top. I wrote to Lord Weinstock [1] the company chairman, outlining my ideas and asking if it was something they might be interested in discussing. To my surprise a couple of days later, I received a phone call from his office asking when I could visit their head office in Borehamwood, Hertfordshire, for a meeting. 'How about tomorrow?' I asked. 'Very well', came the reply, 'we will send a car to the station to meet you.' So, train times were organised and it was agreed I would arrive at Borehamwood Station at 11.00 a.m. the next day.

I was met by the sales manager, Steve, who suggested that we discuss my ideas over lunch in the Director's dining room, where we were joined by their senior program designer, Hal, a man of very few words. His lunch consisted of nothing more than a large cup of strong black coffee. Slightly overawed by the speed at which my ideas were being taken on board and by such an important and progressive company, I briefly explained my requirements.

It was imperative that the current price must appear on all buyers' screens at the same instant whether they were next door or a hundred miles away. One concern I had concerned the scenario of when two buyers may press a bidding key at exactly the same time and that the distance from the auctioneer's main computer to their individual screen may disadvantage the one furthest away. This fear proved groundless, as in the unlikely event of the system receiving both bids simultaneously it would randomly choose only one. In fact as the computer works in speeds of milliseconds it makes a fairer selection than any human auctioneer could.

As we finished lunch Hal, who had been making copious notes while we ate, thought deeply for what seemed an age but was probably about twenty seconds and declared, 'Yes, it can be done, I will write some new software that will adapt our Prestel Service to give you what you need, it will take me about fourteen days.' I am sure he already had in his head the hundreds of programming instructions and calculations that would be required to be written into the new software so as to provide me with my 'computerised remote auction system'.

There would be a number of features, one of which was an on-screen catalogue of individual lots, giving details such as numbers of livestock offered in each 'lot', the weight range, and grading details from previous sales of that particular herd. It would also show both a rolling average and the most recent returns and provide a fair indication of the quality of the stock on offer. I called this the 'Tabrotec Historic Evaluation' or T.H.E. for short. With time, buyers would favour sellers who regularly provided the best and most consistent stock and would bid accordingly.

It was envisaged that the auction would begin at 8.00 a.m. each Friday. At that point I would input a starting price for each lot in turn, falling by one penny per kilo at three second intervals until a bid was received. To bid a buyer would hit a key on his keyboard when he or she accepted the displayed price. At this instant all other buyers would see 'Lot sold' appear in the price box. If no bid was received before the sellers agreed reserve was reached, the lot would be withdrawn.

Steve had arranged that I meet 'the Boss' and give him an outline of my ideas. This I did, taking the opportunity to suggest to Lord Weinstock that GEC may wish to take a financial stake in the project. He declined my offer giving me two reasons: one, that if the idea proved very successful I would eventually regret sharing the ensuing profits with such a large organization; and two, if it wasn't a success then his shareholders would want to know why he had got them involved in livestock auctioneering. My visit ended with the promise that in the next few days they would send me an estimate of the cost of the work involved in creating the system.

My head was spinning as I sat on the train home, because as I hadn't been able to obtain any help from GEC in financing the project, how much would it cost me, and where would I get the money to continue with what I had decided would be called 'The Tabrotec System'. The name Tabrotec was an amalgam of our Taylor Brothers dairy herd prefix which was TABRO and the word Technology. The quote duly arrived giving a figure of £14,000 and a delivery time of 14 days from receipt of my payment and order. This was probably very reasonable even though it worked out at £1,000 per day.

To finance the project I decided to obtain a development grant from the Department of Trade and Industry, making a detailed application setting out the benefits of this method of marketing. A couple of weeks later they replied, turning down my request on the basis that as the DTI did not provide grants for agricultural projects, the marketing of pigs did not come within their terms of reference. Re-applying, I emphasized that the system could be used to sell any product that could be evaluated and described accurately. I explained that the reason for choosing live pigs as the initial product, was that they would give the most effective proof of the benefits of remote auctions, and they were a commodity readily available to me, and of which I had years of valuable marketing experience.

The revised approach was successful, happily, and a substantial grant was made available on the proviso that some investment was required on our part. Spurred on by poor prices for pigs at the local auction markets and prodded by fellow farmers who knew of my ideas and were looking for better returns for their stock, I placed the order with GEC.

Part of the deal required that I receive training on the use of the Prestel System, as I would need to be able to create my catalogue pages on the screen and in the role of auctioneer operate the sales. The training offered would take two days at an additional cost of £300.00 per day plus at least one night in a hotel in London. Add the train fare and it added up to about £750.00, money we could ill afford. As an alternative I asked if it was possible to teach two people over the space of one day instead of one person over two? They agreed and the next week Angela and I caught the early morning train to London arriving at GEC at 9.00 a.m. We were taken straight into the training room and with pens and huge pads of notepaper began a very intensive days' training – after two hours I felt my brain was going to burst. Angela must have felt the same but a short break for tea was all the time that could be spared if we were to complete the two day course in one day. We hoped that if one of us forgot parts of the lesson the other would remember it and then we could piece it all together when we got home. After nine exhausting hours of instruction our brilliant instructor kindly drove us to the station for the return journey and the end of a sixteen-hour day.

The next day, on went the computer and the link via Prestel in to the GEC system and we began creating and editing the pages we intended to use for the catalogue. As we had hoped, the parts of our training that I had forgotten Angela remembered, so with our notes and from memory we gradually built up the framework of the system. Once this was completed we had something to show to prospective buyers and sellers.

I was confident we could find sellers who would try the system as they had nothing to lose and the safeguard of a reserve price would protect them. The buyers would not be so easy to convince for in spite of the advantage of being able to buy without leaving their desks they would need to trust the description of the merchandise. To overcome their misgivings a condition of sale was introduced which stipulated that if there was more than an agreed percentage variation between the catalogue description and the actual stock delivered, they would be permitted to pay on the basis of their current graded price as opposed to the flat rate price bid in the auction. The terms of sale were on an ex-farm basis, so the buyer had to factor in the cost of transportation, just as in the case in traditional livestock markets. This gave a slight advantage to the buyer from an abattoir who was the nearest to the producer's farm and it also proved beneficial from an animal welfare aspect. Twenty-five years on, the latter issue is considered a subject of great importance and commonly known now as 'food miles'.

Data for describing the quality of the pigs was a measurement taken by an optical probe of the thickness of back-fat and rind at a point level with the last rib 6.5cm from the dorsal mid-line; this measurement is called P2 and with the weight of the pig was the main basis of payment by the abattoir. It was then possible to calculate the average weight and P2 of a batch of pigs from any seller. We found that this figure varied very little from the same seller each week and by adding the past three weeks rolling average into the equation a very reliable description of pigs offered was obtained. In a traditional market professional buyers would judge a pen of pigs by 'Skeg of eye' (Yorkshire, for visual appraisal) and a poke with a finger in the P2 position. They would then add their commission, and arrange the haulage, with the latter cost being added to their bill for the abbatoir. If creating Tabrotec did nothing else it showed farmers that they could take more control of the marketing of their pigs and cut out the middle men.

During the setting up of the Tabrotec system at Thirtleby it was soon apparent that we had to apply for an extra telephone line so as to maintain and open line for me whilst running the sale. At first we were told no more lines were available which seemed odd as I had been told by the engineer that there were 40 wires in the cable that came across the fields from the main road. As there were only ten properties in our village, who had all the phones? I discovered much later that as this was at the time the Cold War was at its height, every spare line in Holderness was being used to connect Ministry of Defence bunkers around the coast to radar stations watching for a potential missile attack.

Thus, I decided to go to the top once more or as near the top as I could locally, and duly wrote to the Chairman of Kingston Communications in Hull. I explained, rather cheekily, that as he and I were both in the communications business he would, I was sure, understand my need for an extra line. I suggested he might like to see a demonstration of what I was creating and if he was agreeable, I would bring along some of the buyers and run a mock sale at Telephone House. He couldn't have been more helpful and so we ran such an auction inside Telephone House in Hull with some buyers who came from various parts of the country, together with Steve from GEC. I later got my extra line.

For those who may not know, Kingston Communications is owned by Hull City Corporation who holds the majority share, and is the only one of its kind in the country. Everyone else has BT, we have KC.

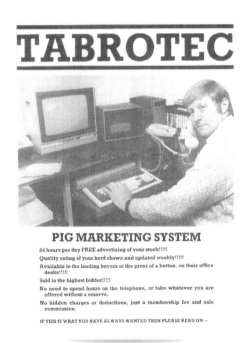

My first promotional leaflet for the Tabrotec system.

Friday, September 1986 at 8.00 a.m., with 300 pigs for sale and three buyers who had agreed to give Tabrotec a try, connected. Monday of that week the details of the pigs in the sale had been entered in the on-screen sale catalogue using recent grading results as a guide to their quality. This first lot was provided by my first seller, local pig producer Peter Kirkwood, who offered 80 pigs. As the weeks progressed the grading information would be updated using returns of the previous three week's sales on the Tabrotec auction. If the pigs delivered varied by more than 5% from the description then the price could be re-negotiated between buyer and seller.

The sale in progress.

I duly entered the starting price on to the screen and every three seconds, and dropped the price by one penny per kilo. Still no bid so another penny per kilo, again no bid but we were still above the reserve although I was getting very nervous, for I certainly did not want the first lot to go unsold. Even though I could not know that the buyer from FMC Meats was determined to be the first to buy on the system and was getting more nervous than me, fearing one of the others would beat him to it, one more penny down and he bid. Success! It worked. The next lot went on screen and the process stated again this time the Sainsbury's buyer did not want to miss out so he bid after only a couple of pence were dropped of the price. Truly, this was open competitive bidding and no 'wheeler dealing'.

Word had got around that Tabrotec was up and running, causing concern among those with a vested interest in maintaining the status quo in livestock marketing. 'Prime Cuts', an abattoir in Hull to whom I had lent a computer terminal, claimed it had been stolen during the Christmas holiday but subsequently logged on to the pre-sale catalogue and attempted to contact the sellers privately to do a deal before the auction. They were quickly barred access. Auctioneers were also showing an interest as they feared being by-passed. Some buyers resisted joining Tabrotec because they enjoyed the ability to 'wheel and deal'. As a small independent operator it was therefore very difficult to recruit enough buyers and sellers to achieve 'critical mass'. The forces of tradition and nervousness to adapt to the relatively new world of computer technology confirmed what even my supporters had said, which was that I was a decade ahead of my time.

Tabrotec operated reasonably successfully for two years although pig numbers never exceeded 400 to 500 per week, thus not reaching the hoped-for 'critical mass' before disaster struck our family.

1 Arnold Weinstock, Baron Weinstock (29 July 1924-23 July 2002), was the son of working class Polish-Jewish immigrants. See http://en.wikipedia.org/wiki/Arnold_Weinstock

Part Two

1. A life-changing tragedy

2 5 August 1988 and our world was suddenly turned upside down. Harvest was late that year and Jonathan was due to go back to school. He was disappointed that we had not started combining and as it was just possible that it would be dry enough to start, I took the combine into the 25 acre field to go once around for a test drive. On the way back on the road past the bungalow going to the barn I saw that Angela had returned in the car with Jonathan and he asked if he could ride on the combine with me. We had travelled only 20 yards when the combine steps hit a roadside stone and he was thrown off and killed. Our lovely 12-year old son. As for his father, who would do anything for him, he could not save him. I know how I felt from that point on but can never know what thoughts must have been going through the minds of his mother, Angela, and his sisters, Helen and Sally.

The next days and weeks were truly dreadful for us all. At Jona's funeral the church was packed with friends and members of the farming community, many of whom said, 'But for the grace of God it could have happened to any of us.' Mr. Sadler, Jona's headmaster from Read School at Drax, gave a short eulogy in church and told us later that there was a moment when he could see Jona' standing in front of him with a cheeky grin on his face as if to say, 'Please don't tell me off Sir.'

That night as we lay in bed I half woke with the feeling that one of the children was sneaking into the bed between us, something they had often done. I felt to see who it was and thought I had touched someone's hair; it seemed like Jonathan's and I remember being half asleep pushing him back down the bed before waking up fully. The thought that I would push any of our children away still hurts to this day. It was so real that I now will believe anybody who says they have had a similar experience. There are some things in life we do not fully understand.

It affected us in many ways. I remember later loading bales on to a trailer with Angela and Helen who did not want us to load more than two bales high as we might fall off. Things I saw other people doing without a second thought seemed to me to be filled with danger. All my ambition for farming and building up Tabrotec came a distant second to caution and safety. I felt it would almost be wrong to be happy when I had caused such sadness even if it had been an accident. Angela could see how much I was hurting and in sympathy she tried to avoid talking about Jonathan, telling the girls not to mention him as it would upset Daddy, but even if it was painful I still wanted to talk about him and not be shielded from what had happened. Again, I couldn't say this as she had done it with the best of intentions but my ability to communicate was being held back by the fear of causing more upset and unhappiness.

To this day I find it physically painful to see anybody cry. So imagine the feeling when Sally, Helen, or Angela was upset for any reason, even a look of sadness on their faces in those days is something I will never erase from my memory.

Though nobody else would have known it, I had for as long as I could remember, and for almost every night before going to sleep, said in my head a very short and simple, silent prayer: 'Please God look after Angela, Sally, Helen, and Jonathan, and all our family, keep them safe and well.' But when Jona' died I lost my faith completely though I do hope others haven't, as it seems to be a great comfort for those who can and do believe.

Only those who have been in this situation can know how it feels and I am reminded of the time a few days after the accident, when the police came to interview me. A young man from Health and Safety arrived at the same time and asked if he could be present during the interview. The policeman agreed providing he just listened and said nothing. Geoff was also present as we sat at the dining room table.

In answer to the police questions I tried to relate the sequence of events as I remembered them, until the man from Health and Safety could contain himself no longer and pointed out: 'Of course Mr. Taylor, you know that Jonathan should not have been riding on the combine in the first place.' He didn't need to remind me, the thought was in my mind every minute of the day and most of the night. For a minute I thought Geoff was going to physically throw him out of the room and both he and the policeman told him that would be the result if he interfered again.

It seemed to me as if an enormous explosion had happened and which had blown a great hole in our family unit for ultimately I could not escape the fact that it had been me who was driving the combine, no matter how many times people said that it was purely an accident. I was responsible for the safety of my children. It must have been worse for Sally, Helen and Angela because where I had only myself to blame, and so kept my anger self-contained, but they probably had to fight two battles; one was the actual loss of a brother and son, the other must have been desperately not wanting to blame me, someone they had trusted. Yet they needed to understand how it could happen if no one was to blame.

My mind was playing tricks with me. Events and things totally unrelated to the accident would find me suddenly re-living in my head the moment it happened until I reached a point when my whole body would convulse; it was as if there was an automatic shut-off, as if my memory would allow me to go no further. This even happened during the night and I would almost jump out of bed as if I had experienced an electric shock. Sometimes the safety shut-off does not work and the flash back is so intense that it takes time to recover. Only someone who has been through a similar trauma can understand or explain how it feels.

For quite a long time when I was alone I would keep the radio or television on all night in my bedroom so as to fill my mind with distractions. Even now I must always have something to do for I can't bear to be totally unoccupied, so I am at my most content when I have a project.

The fact that the girls were growing up and for the best of reasons not at home for much of the time created the feeling that as a family we were all moving in different directions. Helen was soon to be boarding at St Hilda's School in Whitby and Sally was at the beginning of her nursing career in Leeds. The best times for me were when I was bringing them home for the weekends. I could always find my way into Leeds to collect Sally but I don't think I ever found the same route out of the town twice. Driving to and from St Hilda's near Whitby was a much more straight forward affair with the added benefit of some nice countryside to view on the way.

It still concerns me that they would have suffered homesickness on top of everything else. For myself I remember being homesick when I was anything more than 10 miles from home for more than 24 hours.

Those years were a struggle for all of us. There seemed little point hanging on to the farm that we had hoped would be a start in farming for Jonathan. I kept running Tabrotec but throughput never exceeded 500 pigs per week and the maximum number of buyers had peaked at just five, including the local supermarket Jackson's Grandways, who operated an abattoir nearby in Cottingham and were very successful when bidding for local pigs, as their haulage costs were very low – a prime example of the way Tabrotec reduced 'food miles' and consequently stress on the pigs.

GEC who had been most supportive had reached the point when they felt it was necessary to make a charge for the access to their mainframe computer, this being the only way the auction could be run. It was to be several years before the internet came along to provide a facility which would have given me virtually free access to buyers and sellers. The figure GEC quoted was unsustainable for the amount of business I was attracting. The enthusiasm that had fired me into establishing Tabrotec established was now missing in me and investing more money to take it further was not only a daunting prospect but probably foolhardy.

Meanwhile Istel, a company created out of the Information Technology division of motor manufacturer British Leyland, became independent and had a national videotext service which it wished to develop by linking firms like ICI and Hotpoint with their customers. The ICI interest was a service to farmers called Agviser, a development of which brought Istel into direct contact with the farming industry.

Pamela Harman, the Istel project development manager, had heard of Tabrotec, and was aware that it was the only system up and running in Britain of its kind and contacted me in 1988 to arrange a meeting. At the meeting it became obvious that by working together we might be able to overcome some of the resistance that was preventing the expansion of computerised livestock marketing in general, and Tabrotec in particular.

I was later to discover that she had also been talking to traditional livestock market owners who had tried to convince her that computerised livestock marketing as operated by Tabrotec would never work, despite the fact that they were later to set up their own computerised system. I was told the possibility of taking over Tabrotec had been considered, if it became too much of a threat. I wish I had known because there was a time later when I might have accepted a reasonable offer.

Further meetings over several months eventually resulted in the drawing up of a contract between Istel and Tabrotec whereby I would receive a very substantial payment and act as a consultant in a joint venture, and the Tabrotec System would be further developed and operated on the Istel Videotext service. In 1989 the legal department of Istel produced a contract which they offered for approval and signature. I took it to my solicitor David Burnett immediately for scrutiny, and agreeing that it was a very good deal I promptly signed and returned it to Istel for completion with their signature.

During the next week and whilst we were waiting for news that the contract had been signed we received word that though we had made no changes to it, it had to be returned for a final signature to the same legal department who had previously approved it accompanied by their apologies for its delay in its completion. Two weeks later in July 1989 we discovered that Istel had been taken over by AT&T who shelved the £3 million project as being outside their scope of interest. Consequently the delay in the 'legal department' was simply an excuse to gain time while a final decision was made by the new owners – thus, the contract was never signed or returned.

GEC, who had been generous in their support by providing the use of their computer system to run the auctions each week free of charge, now felt we should pay for this service. Though the Tabrotec auction was making a profit it was insufficient to justify the figure they quoted. So with a great deal of regret Tabrotec ceased operating as a computerised auction service.

Shortly after this a farmer friend told me that York Livestock Centre was starting Beacon Electronic Auctions. I was to discover they had been watching the progress of Tabrotec and decided to set up their own system but needed someone to help run it. I gave them a call and was invited for an interview. The day of the interview came around and I was asked to wait in a small room while the directors had a meeting; the interviewing panel comprised leading members of many of the largest livestock auction companies in the country. After a while I was called in to the boardroom and informed that half of them were against the idea of employing me or indeed anybody for the position.

Entering the boardroom I was asked to sit on a large wooden chair on a raised platform facing about 18 people, and as it was no use trying to guess which nine did not want me even to be there I tried to lighten the atmosphere by likening the chair to an electric chair and asked which of them controlled the switch? One member of the interviewing panel seemed more amused by my comment than the others; either that or he was just trying to be friendly. I decided to think it was the latter. It was he who asked the first question. 'Why should we employ you John?' His use of my first name convinced me he was a supporter. My reply was that they needed me because I was the only person who had built and operated such a system in England. They did not ask me many more questions after that, saying they would get in touch in due course. I left convinced I had blown it by being too cocky and phoned Angela at home to report this before heading across to Whitby to bring Helen home for the weekend.

When we got back home Angela told me that Beacon Auctions had phoned asking if I would I return their call as soon as possible. The result was that I started work for Beacon Auctions the following Monday. It differed from Tabrotec in that it was not a Dutch auction with a falling price but a traditional rising bid auction; my objection to this method had been that it was not sufficiently transparent because in a traditional auction the auctioneer could bid. The buyers knew this and so did not totally trust the system. With Tabrotec's Dutch auction only one bid (the first one) could be made.

I stayed at Beacon for nearly three years and quite enjoyed helping to build it up, however I always knew I would outlive my usefulness once it was running successfully, and that eventually cheaper replacements would fill my place. So I left amicably and started to consider my next move.

Angela and I battled on together but eventually and probably not surprisingly she found support elsewhere. Consequently that most important element, trust, had gone out of our lives. You can love someone very much but without trust life together is lived on a on a knife edge, and this is not sustainable over time. It was to become the period in my life when I somehow contrived to do or say the wrong things to Angela, especially when I was trying to explain to her what was going on in my mind. I felt that I didn't deserve to do anything that gave me enjoyment because it would look as though I didn't care about what had brought us to this point in our marriage. Angela said at one time, 'I've lost my old John.' I guess she was right, I certainly wasn't the old me.

Sadly in 1993, and after 18 years, Angela and I divorced after what had been up to then a very happy marriage. I hope that she like me has found happiness. To raise the funds for a fair settlement between us, I sold 40 acres of the land and in addition raised further funds to repay her mother for the money we had borrowed to purchase Geoff's share of the farm.

2
A man's best friends

Many times later when I was alone at home I would have a feeling of helplessness coming over me, when this happened I would go down to the golf club and say to Geoff, 'I'm having a bad time Geoff.' I never needed to say more, he would walk with me around the golf course until the feeling passed over. I am eternally grateful for that support and the similar occasions when the 'treatment' would be performed by cousin Mike and his wife, Carol.

Another most loyal companion who helped to get me through this very dark time in my life was our family Labrador, Honey. She somehow knew when I was feeling down and would sit next to me, put her head on my knee, and just press gently as if to remind me she was there. She was by then a very old dog and I had to take her to the vet several times when she had stiffened up with rheumatism in her back legs. On each occasion I said to the vet please don't be afraid to tell me when it would be unkind to her to keep her going. The vet would say, 'You will know when it is time.'

Some months later when I got up in the morning Honey was laid on her bed at the bottom of the stairs and couldn't stand up. I tried lifting her gently but she was obviously in severe pain. The vet had been right, I would know. Carefully lifting her on her bed into the car I drove the six miles to the vet. Carrying her in to the surgery I just said, 'I think it's time.' They knew what I meant and as I told Honey she was a good dog and stroked her ears she had the injection which took effect in a matter of seconds. I am sure she felt no distress. Nobody said a word. I walked outside and drove home very slowly, tears in my eyes all the way.

Over the next three years I tried offering Bed & Breakfast accommodation, where my breakfasts were legendary; it would have worked very well except for the need to have strangers staying in my house. I was obviously not cut out for the hospitality profession. On one particular occasion a young man who was phoning from a firm in Grimsby on a Friday morning asked if he could book a double room and breakfast for the weekend, and that he expected to arrive at 7.00 p.m. There was a lot of giggling to be heard in the background during the call which I just took to be office banter. That night just before the allotted time of arrival a car pulled into the drive with a young couple who seemed to be having an argument. They took quite a long time to come to the door eventually ringing the bell. When I told them that the double room he had booked was upstairs, the look on the girl's face said it all. She quickly suggested she would first like to go to the pub in the village for a meal. They never returned and I bet it was a very quiet journey when he drove her back to Grimsby.

A few months later my neighbour, Richard Wastling, asked me if I would like to look after his pigs part time? This suited me fine and I think it suited him also because he expanded the numbers and the work became almost full time.

As soon as I reached the grand old age of 65 in July 2002, I retired. Over the years I had breathed in more than enough dust and was beginning to feel the effect of this occupational hazard that can lead to what is known in the industry as 'Farmers Lung'. It was time to turn the page on this chapter of my life.

3

What do farmers do when they retire?

D o Farmers ever retire? The answer in my case is yes, sort of. I retired in 2002 but did not stop working; most farmers find it very difficult to hand over the reins to their sons or daughters. I can just imagine any farmer's son reading this and saying, 'Tell that to my Dad.'

This part of my tale includes amongst other things meeting and marrying Irene, travel, adventure, researching our family history and the unbelievable joy of grandchildren.

Complete retirement didn't last very long before Richard Wastling suggested I might like to do a few runs as part time car driver for John Chichester Constable, the owner of the local stately home Burton Constable Hall. This was an ideal job for me as I love driving, especially when I am being paid for it. 'Mr C' as everybody called him was a most interesting man whom when he inherited the Burton Constable Estate had to cope with the financial fallout of crippling death duties following the death of his father. Over the years he restored the viability of the estate by some very inventive and diverse means, from a mechanical elephant to a hovercraft and the very popular and successful caravan park.

Much of my driving when I was not taking him to London or functions at the Jockey Club in Newmarket would require that I collect house guests from an airport or from London, bringing them up to the Hall and taking them back a week or so later. I met some very interesting people who became good friends, both of us looking forward to the next journey up and down the A1. A particular favourite passenger was Mrs Savoury who as Sheila Brennan, the actress, appeared in the television programmes *Crossroads* and *The Sweeney*, and was Nurse Gladys in the pilot of *Open All Hours* with Ronnie Barker, plus many other films and shows. She was kind enough to laugh at some of my jokes though mostly with a pained expression on her face. I was soon to discover that she and Mr C had over the years developed a private competition when on the road, this entailed seeing who could be the first to spot the most Eddie Stobbart lorries and when one was spotted the winner would shout 'Eddie!' at the top of their voices. It was most unnerving for me as the driver on what had until that moment been a stress free journey, concentrating on the road until the peace was so abruptly shattered.

As with all my passengers, whether I was driving for Mr C or any of his friends, we were just driver and his passenger during the journey, but when the situation arose I would try to act as if I was a professional chauffeur. On one occasion Mr C was sitting in the front seat beside me as we drove down the A1M at the regulation 70 mph (of course), when he suddenly picked up his copy of *The Times* and opened it in all its broadsheet size and dimension fully in front of me, oblivious of the fact that I could not see where I was going. When my natural reaction was to slow down, he said, without looking up from his paper, 'What's the holdup John?' 'Difficulty in seeing the road ahead', I replied. It was a blessing when most newspapers changed to tabloid format.

On another occasion my journey required an overnight stop for us at a Travelodge and on this occasion my passenger had fortified himself on the journey from a bottle of red wine. When at our destination where he was due to have lunch and spend the afternoon with friends, he continued to assuage any potential thirst with liquid replenishments. I, in the meantime, had found a quiet place to park and eat my sandwiches with a flask of tea, acquainting myself with what was to me a brand new vehicle. As our return journey began in the evening we had booked two rooms at another Travelodge, where we enjoyed an evening meal in the restaurant. My passenger ordered wine with his meal saying that he wished to take his time. I, on the other hand, had finished eating and bade him goodnight taking the precaution of asking the waiter to make sure Mr C could find his way to the annexe across the car park. Returning to my room I became concerned that he would not be safe so after about an hour I went outside to check. Fortunately, the waiter and my passenger were just leaving the restaurant arm-in-arm, half a bottle of wine in hand, I dutifully took over thanking the waiter for his help. Much to my embarrassment he grabbed my hand for support. Picture the scene, two elderly gents hand-in-hand, one clutching a half-finished bottle of wine and the other looking extremely shifty scanning the area looking for the deepest shadows, fervently hoping nobody would see us staggering across the car park. The next morning he emerged from his room full of life whereas I who had had nothing stronger than orange juice emerged from mine glad to forego breakfast and get back on the road.

Meeting Irene

In 1995 I met Irene. Though Irene did not ski, our mutual friend Jenny had persuaded her to go to one of our local ski club summer meetings, which as usual began with a short walk and ended in a pub; with the benefit of hindsight it is now obvious that Jenny had serious matchmaking in mind. Jenny was always the one to tie up any loose ends and I think in her eyes I was one such loose end. Of course to tie up loose ends you need another loose end so who better than her friend Irene. It wasn't until 1997 that we began a long engagement period. The reason for the long engagement was that whilst working I needed to continue living at Thirtleby while Irene worked in Hull and her flat in

Cottingham was most convenient for her. Our plan was that when I retired we would sell both properties and make a fresh start somewhere which suited us both.

Life since meeting Irene has changed completely for, whilst we come from quite different backgrounds she has opened my eyes to a great many new experiences.

She is a great cook and we laugh about the fact that some of her specialties have the same name but not necessarily the same ingredients every time. It is a similar situation with our holidays, no matter how simple they seem in the planning the outcome is always an adventure. In the early ones I could have been excused for thinking she had secretly planned for some sort of disturbance to occur in the country we were visiting. For instance, there was always at some point a turnout of the military or the state police, such as the time in Russia when the Mafia interfered with our visit to the Moscow State Circus or in Vienna when tanks and soldiers blocked our entrance to one of the State Museums.

Irene changed my life for the better for which I am eternally grateful, as I hope are my family and friends who must have been getting pretty despairing of ever getting me back on track. I hope she has the best bits of the Old John with a few improvements added. It is for others to say what the worst bits are which still remain.

Before introducing us, Jenny and I amongst others, had been a founder members of the White Star Ski Club. I particularly remember with fondness, the weekend years before, when we had held a BBQ in the barn at Thirtleby to raise funds for the new club. The event was a roaring success so much so that we almost melted my mother's cooker pre-cooking about 200 chicken portions before finishing them off on the BBQ. We were very nervous of poisoning anybody at such an early stage in the club's formation.

Restoring the Jaguar Mk 2

In 1994, a year before meeting Irene, I had purchased a 1964 Jaguar Mk 2 for restoration. The car had been advertised in the *Yorkshire Post* for several weeks at a price of £2,500 so with next door neighbour Andy, we headed off to the dealer in Huddersfield to view it. When we arrived it was covered in dust in the corner of the garage wedged in behind several other classic cars. With the application of a battery the engine started but they couldn't move it without moving about six other cars first, also they said that the clutch had gone but still offered to pull it out. However, I saw this as a bargaining advantage so said not to bother we would just have a look at the side we could see, and also look at some of the other cars in the showroom.

Appearing suitably uninterested we wandered around for a few minutes during which I wrote out a cheque for £1,600 which I dropped in at the office and said, 'I will have the Jag if you will deliver it to me, if not just tear up the cheque and we will leave it at that.' He looked at the cheque and said, 'I can't drop £900.00 on it!' I said, 'Ok', and walked away, but before we even got to Andy's car he came after us and said, 'How far we have to go to deliver it?' I replied, 'Just along the M62 to Thirtleby', and left it to him to discover how far it actually was.

The whole weekend I was wondering just what I had done, we hadn't even seen the passenger side of the car, or how bad might the clutch be and was that the only reason why it couldn't be moved? But at last on Monday it arrived and we were actually able to drive it off the transporter and into my garage.

The Jag before

... during

... and after.

Fourteen months of welding, scraping, and painting and we took it to a Classic car show at Castle Howard. We didn't win a prize but just sat next to it in the sunshine drinking a toast to 112 DXF.

Some of the events we entered.

Entente Cordiale Tour with the Jaguar Enthusiasts Club

Irene and I toured France on the Jaguar Enthusiasts Club's 1999 Entente Cordiale Tour to the Champagne Region of France, a tour which included a visit to the cellars of Moet & Chandon. On the drive down to Dover we had our first and only breakdown. With 30 miles to go for the day the red charge warning light came on as we pulled into a service station. At that stage we had not joined the Jaguar Enthusiasts Club tour group so did not have the benefit of the two support cars full of spares which would later accompany the tour group's cars. Calling the AA a patrol of which we had seen at the other side of the car park, we requested assistance but as we were not the next on the list for assistance the AA van drove straight past us. We waited almost an hour for him to return and when he did he told me the dynamo wasn't charging. I knew that already and as he had no other suggestion to make we decided to press on and hope the battery would hold out until we reached Dover. We should have done this in the first place as it was now getting dark and I did not want to use my lights for fear of flattening the battery completely.

Dover 1999, playing with the Big Boys en route to France.

As we arrived at the hotel in Dover and parked, two chaps who were admiring all the old Jaguars came to look at ours. I told them of our plight and one said, 'What time do you sail tomorrow?' '11.30 a.m.', I replied. 'Right', he said, 'I will meet you here at 7.30 a.m. and take you and the dynamo to a friend of mine in Dover, he will fix you up.' Next morning I removed the dynamo with the help of the tour mechanics and true to his word we took it to his friend's workshop in Dover. With a quick glance at the dynamo the owner said, 'I am sure we have some carbon brushes to fit that, they are in a box somewhere in the loft.' After a lot of rummaging about in boxes he found two, and they fitted the brushes and cleaned and tested the dynamo, steadfastly refusing any payment. Nonetheless, I gave him £20.00 and the same to the Good Samaritan who had arranged it all. We dashed back to the car park where Irene was anxiously waiting with the two tour mechanics who duly refitted the dynamo in record time, enabling us to join the parade of Jaguars by slipping in behind the police car escorting us all to the ferry.

The tour of the cellars of Moet & Chandon included a five course dinner actually eaten in the champagne cellars during which we were shown what was the correct champagne to drink with each course and not just a taste, for every time you drank some they would refill it immediately, thus explaining why there were five glasses at each place setting.

Down in the champagne cellars ready to commence dinner.

Not likely to run out of champagne on the night.

A drive around the old Reims motor racing circuit gave us an opportunity to hear the roar of our Jaguar's engine as we flashed past the pits. The circuit was due for demolition later that month so we may have been the last ones to race round it. We finished the trip off by leaving the tour group and more importantly the support vehicles, to drive through Paris and its rush hour traffic, particularly hair raising were the five lanes in each direction going down the Champs-Élysées and around the Arc de Triomphe. The secret was not to let them see the fear in my eyes. We survived Paris without a scratch and continued on our way to visit Monet's Garden at Giverny. Though the sun was shining as we arrived and entered the turnstiles, on emerging at the other side two seconds later, it was raining, yet this had the beneficial effect of heightening the fragrance of the flowers.

Beautiful Giverny, even in the rain.

For our last two nights in France we had booked to stay at a chateau near Giverny. Arriving at 5.30 p.m. we wondered why there were no other cars in the car park. We took our bags to the door to find it locked so rang the bell and after what seemed an age it creaked open. Declaring who we were and that we had booked a room the gentleman asked us to follow him up a very grand staircase in one of the four towers situated at each corner of the building – noticeably he did not offer to carry any of the bags.

We climbed four floors into our rooms at the very top of the tower. We had an en-suite bedroom but were shown in to an enormous bedroom which adjoined an even larger bathroom, complete with a roll top bath in the middle of the floor accompanied by a toilet and bidet at the other side of the room.

When I asked what time they served dinner I was told that as we were the only guests the chef would not be coming in this week but his cousin had a very nice restaurant in the nearby village and if we were quick we might be in time to get a meal there. We arrived in time but even this establishment was a bit like the Marie Celeste – what did everybody else know that we didn't know? In spite of this, we were made welcome and presented with the menu, in French naturally. We started with soup based on the theory that you cannot go far wrong with soup, it was excellent whatever it was. We had chosen a fish dish for the main course and when it arrived it was French cuisine at the extreme end of the scale. Very rich with loads of cream sauce deluged on prawns and every other kind of fish imaginable, in fact it was so full of rich goodness that Irene was ill most of the night. The bill was enough to give me indigestion as well.

We only stayed one night in the dark and otherwise deserted chateau of four towers, seeing the proprietor for only the second time to pay the bill. True to form we lugged our own suitcases down the stairs. I bet there was a lift somewhere but that might have cost extra and used more of the obviously scarce electricity.

Back to Calais and the ferry to Dover for an uneventful drive home with some great memories especially as the Jaguar had served us so well.

Life in Hornsea

Life in Hornsea is very enjoyable and we knew we were becoming accepted when the chemist knew our names as soon as we walked through the door. In fact we didn't need to ask for our prescriptions, they were handed to us as soon as we approached the counter.

The drive into Hornsea from either direction is always welcoming, with the Mere seen through the trees when coming from the west or from the top of the hill when arriving from the south.

I well remember that particular Hill had taken on a new dimension many years ago when I offered to use my Jeep to tow a low-loader carrying an ex-army DKW (Duck); the weight of Low loader and DKW combined must have been about six tons and the jeep only one and a half tons. I had towed it from Hull forgetting the hill by the side of the mere until I arrived at the top of it, there was nothing I could do but to engage low ratio bottom gear and four-wheel drive and cross my fingers. Unsurprisingly, we gathered speed relentlessly with a T-junction getting ever closer, the little jeep engine was screaming in protest until we slowed to about 30mph and a merciful lack of approaching traffic at the junction enabled me apply some power to start the jeep pulling rather than being pushed, successfully turning the corner and most importantly keeping the jeep in front of the trailer.

4

Russia –
'The Cruise of the Tsars'

I rene and I had our first taste of serious travel in July 1997 when we flew to St Petersburg in Russia for a river cruise entitled 'The Cruise of the Tsars'. It followed the rivers, lakes and canals to its end in Moscow. Arrival in St Petersburg became a little stressful when none of our luggage appeared on the carousel and things got even worse when they switched most of the lights off and the only other person left in the building was a cleaning lady. As we had no idea where the ship was docked and there was no sign of our travel guide we left the building without realizing we may have entered Russia illegally by not going through customs, who also seemed to have gone home for the day.

In the coach park we spotted a bus in the process of leaving and recognized on board two people who we had seen back in Manchester Airport, flagging it down we discovered it was our bus, told the courier of our plight and she escorted us to the lost luggage office where things didn't improve when we realized she did not speak the same dialect as the people behind the desk. After describing what our luggage looked like with the aid of a book of photos of every imaginable kind of luggage, we were told by a mixture of sign language and facial expressions that it was probably still in Manchester and would perhaps arrive in two days, at least we hoped that is what they were saying.

On board our cruise ship the *Zosima Shashkov* word of our plight soon circulated and the ladies began offering Irene loans of new underwear while I was offered only deodorant and other items. I tried not to dwell on the reasoning behind this apparent choice of what I suited my requirements preferring to believe that none of the other men on board had brought any unused or spare underwear.

Zosima Shashkov.

Peterhoff, the Summer Palace.

Three days later our guide received a telephone message from the airport that our bags were ready for collection but whilst she and I were on a wild goose/taxi-driver chase to the airport to collect the longed for luggage, it arrived at the ship via a battered old bus. Mind you all the busses were battered so I guess they could find nothing better. Two hours after our return the ship set sail down the river Neva towards Lake Ladoga. Located in north western Russia, directly east of St. Petersburg and to the southeast of Finland, Lake Ladoga is Russia's largest freshwater lake. After visiting several Islands in the lake we headed for the Svir River.

The 139 mile long Svir flows from Lake Ladoga east to Lake Onega, connecting the two largest lakes of Europe. A visit to Kitsi Island in Lake Ladoga was held up when President Yeltsin decided to go fishing. We had to wait offshore for three hours until his helicopter had taken him back to his Dacha or weekend retreat. Once on the island we visited the beautiful wooden Church of the Transfiguration.

The Church of the Transfiguration

The Church of the Transfiguration is a beautiful and amazing building. It is constructed completely without nails. The wooden shingles are made of aspen which is capable of reflecting several hues. The midday sun makes them shimmer like gold or silver and the dawn or dusk light turns them a rich purple. Supposedly on fixing the final shingle the master carpenter, a man named Nestor, hurled his axe into the lake proclaiming, 'There never was nor ever will be such a building again'.

Evenings on board *Zosima Shashkov* included Russian language lessons, and on one occasion a competition in which Irene and I had to perform a short mime play, followed by me singing 'On Ilkley Moor Bah't at'. The other contestants were so bad that we won the second prize.

Some of the visits to the small towns were real eye openers, the shops had very little stock on display and it was a very convoluted process when wanting to buy. We gave our guide the slip one day and went into a not-so super supermarket.

The local Supermarket

In the supermarket that we visited there were no window displays to be seen at all, in fact there was no glass only steel sheets painted grey or rust, not a rusty colour just rusty. Even though it was quite dark inside no lights were switched on with the only light radiating from two heavily barred windows at the back. The buying procedure involved spotting what you wanted on the shelves behind the counter before asking the assistant if you could have it, or in our case pointing to it and saying, 'Please.' You were then given a chitty which you took over to another girl at a till, though it wasn't a till it was a box with an abacus next to it. Once you handed over your chitty and paid for the goods, it was then stamped and given back to you to take to assistant number one who would study it carefully before handing over your purchase.

Super supermarket.

We next headed south through a massive lock and into the Rybinsk Reservoir, which is nicknamed 'The White Sea', as it is one of the greatest artificial bodies of water in the world. Locks were built as part of Stalin's plan in 1935 to make Moscow an inland port. The water surface area of the reservoir is over 4.5 square kilometres and it has a depth as much as 26 metres. The waves on 'The Sea' can reach up to a height of two to three metres.

'The Sea' originated following the 1935 decision to build the Uglitch and Rybinsk hydroelectric power plants on the Volga River. Many thousands of Stalin's prisoners were forced to work on the scheme which resulted in the ancient city of Mologa, and more than seven hundred surrounding villages being totally submerged. Around 130,000 displaced people had to be resettled as a result of the 'The Sea' being built.

The Moscow Canal

As the cruise progressed we made our way into the Moscow Canal, where local historians estimate the death toll during its construction was within the range of 700,000 to 1,500,000 people. Most likely, that latter figure is an exaggeration. However, what is known from the stories told by the witnesses is that the lists of the people to be shot were very long – whole sheets of paper with the resolutions 'to shoot', and a single illegible signature.

One incident from this time stands out. On 4 July 1934, Joseph Stalin visited the construction site. Observing the foundation pit, he noticed that the inmates were working barefoot. Even though it was in summer, the weather was not very warm. Stalin immediately interrogated his retinue – the directors of the project – 'Why have the workers no footwear?' They stalled, saying that they had to bring too many workers on the site, and footwear was on the way. Stalin abruptly ordered the footwear to be delivered within two hours, and several men in charge of the provision to be shot. They were shot immediately and thrown into the ditch were they stood.

We ended the holiday in Moscow with a promised visit to the famous State Circus and although we sat in the auditorium for over an hour, was eventually cancelled despite the orchestra turning up and playing one tune before standing up and leaving. We did get our money back and was told off the record that 'powerful forces' had not been paid and as a result no performance would take place until the situation was remedied. Was this Russian Mafia protection money? It is likely that we will never know.

5

Researching the ancestors

I should explain what it was that convinced me to write this book. One day when I was researching our family history on the internet, I realised how much easier it would have been if earlier generations of my family had left a written record chronicling, what may have seemed to them unimportant events in their lives at the time, but to me, now, were tantalising hints of their personal history, and raised questions I was unable to answer.

My research had taken me back as far as 1771 and the birth in London of my great-great-great Grandfather Robert Taylor, who became a Master Mariner. His wife Nancy died in Russell Street in Hull in 1851 at the age of 81, and in the Census of that year she was described as being a 'House Inspector', and that she apparently worked until the very year of her death.

Robert and Nancy had a son, Thomas, born in Stepney, London, on 11 July 1811. In 1881 he married Eliza Dickon who was born in Hull in 1831. Eliza's brother, John, had sailed to Philadelphia on the *S.S. William Penn* in 1848. What intrigues me is why he left his father John, who was a cabinet maker in his own right in English Street, Hull, and who owned three freehold houses in Grimsby Lane, thereby entitling him to vote, as shown on the Electoral Register of 1834. Obviously he had been a man of substance in the town. The name Dickon appears later when it is used as my Grandfather's middle name, probably as a tribute to the Dickon family with whom his father Robert had lodged for a number of years.

I believe that Thomas must have continued the family sailing theme as he had one son Robert, born July 1834 in Accrington in Lancashire, along with three daughters: Eliza born in Hull in 1838, Jemima Flint born in Liverpool in 1843, and Mary born in Hull in 1849. Was he sailing between Hull and Liverpool during these years?

Intriguingly, in 1856 Robert married Mary Griffiths, born in 1832 in Buckley Flintshire, and they were married in Birkenhead St Mary. Robert would be nine years old when his sister Jemima was born and given the middle name Flint; she would be christened when the person who was later to become her auntie was 11 years old. My tentative supposition is that Robert and Mary's parents and the Griffiths family were good friends, Flintshire and Liverpool not being far apart. Robert and Mary Griffith were only two years apart in age. Did they start as playmates aged nine and 11 when Jemima was born and go on to marry in 1856 at the ages of 22 and 24 respectively? Was Jemima given the middle name Flint as a tribute to the longstanding friendship between the two families? That would be a very heart-warming answer to an intriguing question.

Thomas's perambulations between Hull and Liverpool were exceeded by his son Robert, who according to the 1861 census had followed the family tradition and was a Mariner, and his wife Mary, who had two daughters and three sons: the first-born was Murray in 1858 in Birkenhead in Cheshire; next was George W. in 1864 on Chios Island, Turkey (British Subject), followed by my grandfather John Dickon in 1865 also on Chios Island (B.S.), and Virginia born 1869 on Chios Island (B.S.). Finally back in England, Percy William was born in Hull in 1873. The nagging question here is what were Robert and Mary doing on Chios between 1861 and 1873? If only I had been older when Grandfather John Dickon Taylor was alive I could have asked him. But you could also say why didn't I ask my father? The answer is that we do not consider these things important until we are older and then it is often too late.

The unanswered questions continued on my Mother's side beginning in 1752 with a John Monseair reputed to be from a line of Huguenot immigrants who had fled France by the end of the seventeenth and early eighteenth century due to a series of religious persecutions; during this period an estimated half a million Huguenots left France. They immigrated to Protestant nations such as England and the Netherlands. As far as I can tell their French names would originally have included the name of the town or village of their birth, an example would be Monsieur Tours for a man from Tours. This would then be anglicised by dropping the town name and in our case changing Monsieur to become the surname Monseair, or John Monseair.

(left) Grandpa and Grandma Harvey; (right) Grandpa Taylor, my mother, and Grandma Taylor.

I remember my paternal grandfather John Dickon Taylor as a very old man sitting in front of the fire at our bungalow in Ganstead smoking a pipe; my mother had usually put an old rug or sheet under and around his chair to catch the stray tobacco which inevitably fell about him. He had been a boat builder in Hull and one of some considerable repute as I discovered one day when with my then girlfriend Judy Bates we delivered a Christmas gift parcel for Judy's Mum – it was from the Towns Women's Guild for an old gentleman living in the Salvation Army Hostel in Hull. Arriving at his room in the hostel we knocked on the door and were invited into his dark and not very warm accommodation. The man, who lived alone, asked if we could reach the electricity meter high up on the wall to put his few coins in, for he normally stood on a rickety old three legged stool, and the two shilling pieces enabled him to switch the light on again.

He was obviously eager that we should stay and keep him company because he built up the fire which had almost gone out, with a shovel full of coke seeming to have been standing by for just such an occasion. We sat down and explained the reason for our visit whilst handing him the parcel. By way of conversation I asked him what his job had been when he was working, he replied that he had worked in the shipbuilding industry all his life from leaving school. I told him my grandfather John Dickon Taylor had been a boat builder in Hull. His immediate response was 'John Taylor, I was apprenticed to him, he was the finest boat builder in England'. What an amazing coincidence that we should deliver that one food parcel for Judy's mother to a man who had worked and learned his trade under the guidance of my Grandfather.

There must be many more hidden stories like this in everyone's family not just mine, although you have to be prepared for some very sad events which may be laid bare.

My Parents

My father fought in the 1914-1918 war and served in Salonika. In 1915, a large Allied expeditionary force established a base at Thessaloniki for operations against pro-German Bulgaria. This led to the establishment of the Macedonian Front, also known as the Salonika Front. He was gassed at some point in the war, with the gas destroying one of his lungs in the process, and that he had been more or less given up for dead with the trumpeter being called out to play the last-post. Fortunately he recovered just in time for the trumpeter to be stood down before he had played a note.

Dad on his horse.

He served in the East Yorkshire Yeomanry during the First World War and like most men in that conflict did not tell us much about his experiences. One thing I can remember is him trying to teach us to speak to each other by whistling. It was only quite recently that I watched a television programme about how in Thessaloniki during the war the Greek guerillas fighting against the pro-German Bulgarians used to communicate by whistling. One of the Greek men interviewed demonstrated this and it was exactly the same as Dad had tried to teach us but without ever divulging where he had first learnt to do it.

My mother and father on their wedding day, Hull, 1925.

In my parent's wedding photograph (above) there is a notice on the wall behind them that contains the words 'Three Millions of Slaves'. I cannot decipher the rest but it must have caused some concern or amusement when the photos were later developed.

Mum's father, my Grandpa Harvey, was an engineer and worked for Reckitts in the Hull Canister Works. Apparently this came about when Mr Reckitt visited the coal mine near Wakefield where Grandpa worked at the time. Mr Reckitt was so impressed by my Grandpa's work that he told him if he ever wanted to move to Hull he could work for him.

Mum was 24 and Dad 31 when they married in Hull living at first in the Garden Village, an estate built for the workers at Reckitts; later they bought a new bungalow on the outskirts of Hull in Ganstead Lane. My brother Geoff was born in 1931 while they were living in the Garden Village and I

(back row) Grandpa Luke Harvey, his father George, (landlord)
and George Jnr., in front of the Bay Horse, Hall Green, Crigglestone,
near Wakefield, c. 1895.

was born in 1937 when we lived in Ganstead. Two years later World War
Two broke out – I claim that no cause and effect should be assumed here

Now we move to more recent times and into the wonderful phase of
being a grandparent and hearing that magical word 'Granddad' for the first
time. New additions to our family tree are my first grandchild, Jessica, born
on 11 December 1998, the eldest of two daughters of my daughter, Sally,
and her husband Adam Norris, and Emily Norris, born 23 September 2000.
Both children were born in Cambridge. To my daughter, Helen, and her
husband Alan Ansell, a daughter, Keira Mae was born on 28 September
2010, and a son, Harry Orson, born on 14 April 2013. Both children were
born in Edinburgh.

Sally had asked me sometime during 2000 to choose whether I would
like to be called Grandpa or Granddad? I opted for Granddad as it seemed
the logical extension of Dad. She then tried to explain to Jessica and Emily
how children called the same person Granddad that she called Dad. That

led her to explain that I had only become her Dad when her mother Angela married me and I adopted her. The inevitable question that followed was, 'So is he a proper Granddad?' From that day on I was known as 'Proper Granddad'. It gave me a great feeling of pride when one day I unexpectedly picked them up from school and Emily saw me at the school gate and shouted excitedly to Jessica, 'Jess, it's "Proper Granddad"'. So I was 'Proper' and I could wish for no greater accolade than that.

Recently, Helen and Alan's three year-old daughter, Keira shouted to me from the bathroom, 'Granddad, come and watch me wash my hands'. To be considered so special so as to be invited to see what a clever girl she was brings a lump to my throat. On reflection I could have been called upon for a less enjoyable experience, but even then the feeling of being special would have been just the same. I am waiting now for the moment when her little brother Harry calls me Granddad for his first time. Of such things are the most treasured memories made.

'Three generations.'
Left to right: Sally, Jessica, Harry, John, Keira, Emily and Helen.

6

Back to
our adventures

In 1998 we flew to Vancouver, Canada, with Mike and Carol for a touring holiday in a hired car. The aim was to tour the Rockies before staying a few days in Calgary and attending the famous Calgary Stampede and parades.

Before leaving Vancouver we took the ferry to Victoria, first having High Tea, a time honored tradition for over a century. The world renowned tea lobby of The Fairmont Empress has served England's most beloved ritual and Victoria's grandest tradition of Afternoon Tea to royalty, celebrities and now to the four of us. Surrounded by antique tapestries and rugs, sitting in wing back chairs, at a hand-carved table, was an experience for all who enjoy Afternoon Tea. Just like 'Bettys' in York but not as busy.

The Pastry Chef and his team serve hand-made signature Empress Scones, delectable pastries and tea sweets prepared in house daily. From the original blend of The Empress Tea created specifically for The Fairmont Empress, served in dainty William Edwards (formerly Booth and Royal Doulton), china and the sterling silver service ambiance of the live piano, Afternoon Tea is an absolute 'must do' on a visit to Victoria. Before catching the ferry back to the mainland we visited the Butchart Gardens which in July was the most colourful time to see the roses.

Buchart Gardens.

Back in Vancouver we discovered a connection with Hull and Yorkshire in the area known as Gastown, named after 'Gassy' Jack Deighton, born in Hull, Yorkshire in 1830, he died in Gasstown in May, 1875. He had been a steamboat captain and bar keeper who arrived in Canada in 1867 with six dollars and a barrel of whiskey.

(left) 'Gassy' Jack (standing on the barrel) and Mike;
(right) Gastown Steam Clock.

He persuaded workers at the local sawmill to build him a bar in return for free whiskey and within 24 hours his bar 'The Globe' was built enabling him to open the area's first saloon, selling the rest of the barrel of whiskey to the loggers who had flooded into the region. The name 'Gassy' is thought to derive from his constant storytelling and talkative nature. 'Gassing' as we would say in Yorkshire.

The steam clock weighs two tons and stands on top of a vent that is part of the area heating system; operated by the steam it chimes on the hour and quarter hour.

A day whale watching on the Sound was amply satisfied when we encountered a pod of about twenty orcas giving us a fantastic display of breaching completely out of the water before diving under the boat and re-appearing at the other side.

Irene and the author in Vancouver – two very happy tourists.

Heading into the Rockies we negotiated about 50 miles of gravel track to our next stop at a timber lodge on the edge of a lake.

The track to Tyacks Mountain Lodge.

Tyacks Wilderness Resort and Mountain Lodge.

It was a wonderful place and after our precarious drive we then discovered that the best way to get there was by float plane which landed directly in front of the lodge. However, even the drive was an experience we would not have wanted to miss for it was certainly memorable. I suppose the 'Wilderness' in the name should have given us a clue as to the nature of the access road.

Better to have a bear in front than a bare behind.

In the National Park near Jasper we spotted a black bear in the bushes at the side of the road eating berries and stopping the car I opened the side door and started filming it. With my left eye closed and my right eye to the viewfinder I carefully tracked it as it padded slowly along, until a foot appeared in the bottom of the picture about ten inches from its nose while it munched another mouthful of blueberries. Almost too late the brain cells kicked in and I recognised the foot as mine withdrawing it and sliding the door shut with the speed of reaction that only fear can generate.

It was on this day we came to the conclusion that Irene had what we called an 'aura', which had the power to draw wild animals from their hiding places. On one occasion as we were taking a stroll along the road above a mountain stream, a wolf on the opposite river bank trotted into view with its grey head down, totally oblivious to our presence. It was only in view for a few seconds and its grey/brown coat matched the surroundings so perfectly that without Irene's 'aura' we would never have spotted it, before it disappeared into the forest.

Over the next weeks we continued on our way through the Rockies stopping at Jasper, Lake Louise and driving along the Icelands Parkway to Calgary arriving at the beginning of the Stampede.

Calgary Stampede is an annual rodeo, exhibition and festival held every July in Calgary, Alberta, Canada. The ten day event, which bills itself as 'The Greatest Outdoor Show on Earth', had been something I had wanted to visit for many years and as it coincided with my birthday it was a great way to spend a few days. It attracts over one million visitors and features one of the world's largest rodeos, a parade, midway, stage shows, concerts, agricultural competitions, chuck wagon racing and First Nations exhibitions. 'First Nations Canadians' is I think a very nice collective name used to describe the tribes who inhabited Canada before the arrival of predominately white settlers.

Organized by thousands of volunteers and supported by civic leaders, the Calgary Stampede had grown into one of the world's richest rodeos, one of Canada's largest festivals and a significant tourist attraction for the city. Rodeo and chuck wagon racing events are televised across Canada. The city takes on a party atmosphere during Stampede. Office buildings and storefronts are painted in cowboy themes, residents don western wear and events held across the city include hundreds of pancake breakfasts and barbecues. Irene and I got up early one morning and went down to the main street in the banking area where we sat on bales of straw eating bacon and sausages followed by pancakes covered with lashings of maple syrup and all provided free by the staff of the bank we happened to be near.

As we wandered down the street a parade of the various tribes of First Nation Canadians in full traditional dress with their horses, some mounted, some running loose, came past on what had originally been the Blackfoot trail and were heading for their encampment in the showground.

It was whilst walking around this camp the following day that I was suddenly overcome by the realisation of how much Jona would have enjoyed this experience. The feeling was quite overwhelming and I suddenly burst into tears, yet carried on walking hoping it would not be noticed, but both Irene and Mike realised something was wrong. I explained what had happened and they as usual understood and sympathised until I regained my composure. Coming completely out of the blue it hit me very hard that day.

The Chuck Wagon Races.

For our second day we had booked to see the whole rodeo show which included lunch in the main stand in the late afternoon followed by a spectacular night time stage show performed on a huge stage transported to the front of the stand on dozens of independently steerable wheels mounted on jumbo jet-like undercarriages and pulled in by a massive double tyre four-wheel drive John Deere Tractor.

(left) Taking the bull by the horns Calgary-style; (right) wrangling a steer.

(Courtesy of http://www.viewcalgary.com)

The rodeo began with demonstrations of steer wrangling as cowboys or cowgirls on horseback either lasso or chase down steers before jumping down and wrestling them to the ground, while with a movement so quick you can hardly see how they do it, they tie the animal's four feet together. The whole operation only takes a few seconds and the steers are none the worse for it as they lie quite pacified. A clown pretending to be a novice rider then gave a display of trick riding showing that he was definitely not a novice.

The famous chuck wagon races comprised four teams with wagons, with each wagon being pulled by four horses and attended by two or three outriders. The aim being that at the sound of a starting bell, the stove and its pots and pans are packed into the chuck wagon before racing at full gallop around a one-mile course at high speed to return back to the arena where they then unpack and light the stove. The winning team is the first to get smoke issuing from the chimney of the stove. As we had endured a massive rain storm with thunder and lightning during the lunch break, temporarily flooding the whole arena and race track, this proved to be no mean feat.

Stampede Stage Show.

There was so much to see in Calgary including a visit to the Saddle Dome Arena, so called because of the saddle-shaped roof, we were taken to the top deck seats from which vantage point workmen and articulated lorries below on the arena floor looked like mechanised dinky toys as they prepared for the next event.

All too soon the time came to leave our top floor luxury apartment to return the hire car to the depot at the airport and check-in for the flight back home to England and normal life, with such mundane tasks to attend to, as in my case, a longstanding hospital appointment.

Home... and a funny thing happened on the way to the theatre

I had arrived for my appointment to find the waiting room of the X-ray department at the Westwood Hospital in Beverley deserted except for the receptionist, who without taking her eyes off the obligatory computer screen said a cheery good morning. Agreeing that it was indeed morning and up to that point quite good, I introduced myself, giving details that were confirmed on the computer screen. So despite the apparent lack of activity at least I was expected. Little did I know that before the morning was out I was going to re-enact one of those nightmares when you dream you are in a public place wearing, at best, only your pyjamas or at worst nothing at all.

Almost immediately, I was collected by a nurse and ushered through two swing doors into a short corridor, immediately on one side of which were three small changing cubicles. It was in the first of these that I was instructed to remove all my clothes, and put on the regulation hospital gown, although it was suggested I should keep my socks on, a pity that for, at the time my feet may well have been my most attractive feature. The nurse then left asking me to give her a call when I was ready.

Inside the cubicle a notice instructed patients to wear the gown with the opening at the back but unfortunately the one provided for me was far too small and failed to circumnavigate my torso completely, leaving a six inch gap at the back. Now I am not particularly overweight and could not believe that there were no larger gowns available but as I was now completely naked except for the permitted socks, it seemed imprudent to call the nurse back for a replacement. I have since heard that it is not unknown for nurses to plan these little japes to brighten up an otherwise quiet day.

In these circumstances there was no alternative but to struggle into the gown, call the nurse and make sure no one followed me when I ventured out from the cubicle, so with some trepidation I stepped out into the corridor, where to my horror not six feet behind me someone had wedged wide open the doors into the now extremely busy waiting room. I pulled back my shoulders in a vain attempt to close the gap in my now dangerously inadequate attire. The cold draught and sudden silence emanating from the waiting room told me all I needed to know about the situation. I hoped my blushes had been restricted to my face and not extended to the region now visible to the occupants of the waiting room. Fate then struck another savage blow. A gust of wind blew through the doors causing the gown to billow out in front of me much like a yacht flying a spinnaker. I was still fighting to control the errant white nylon when mercifully we reached the sanctuary of the X-ray facility.

There then began what I was told was a 'procedure' that involved being connected to a compressor and inflated through the appropriate orifice to an unspecified pressure, using a mixture of air and an X-ray reflective gas. This explained why the gown should be open at the back. During the procedure I was rotated much like a pig on a roasting spit whilst being X-rayed from every conceivable angle. Noticing that I was looking rather hot and bothered the nurse opened a window near my head, this coincided with a warning that they were about to release the pressure. I was now laid at an angle of thirty degrees or so, aimed directly at the open window much like a rocket on the launch pad. The nurse hastily grabbed my feet as the air line was disconnected as she too had seemingly spotted the danger.

To put it politely the natural processes involved in returning me to barometric equilibrium with the atmosphere created a situation where I could imagine being propelled through the window, out over the hospital car park in a random spiraling trajectory, leaving the nurse holding nothing more than a pair of smouldering socks. Horror of horrors, I might have even emitted the sort of noises produced by accidently released party balloons! Thankfully, the nurse's grip held and I stayed firmly and silently on the 'launch pad' as the procedure was completed successfully.

Dismounting the 'rotisserie' and returning to the changing cubicle I was relieved to see that the waiting room doors had by now been properly closed. Confidence returned with the thought that the occupants would surely not be the same ones who had witnessed my earlier exposure; in any case they had not seen my face or the clothes that I was now wearing. I was grasping at straws of course but with this in mind I confidently entered the waiting room to be met by smiles and knowing looks and the same sudden ominous silence that had accompanied my walk of shame half an hour before. What had given the game away? Surely it couldn't be my face that was now almost as red as my hair?

7

My contribution to family connections with the sea

With nine friends we chartered two yachts in 2000 to sail around the British Virgin Islands in the Caribbean and as our party comprised two qualified skippers we decided they should skipper a boat each, sharing the rest of our motley crew between them. Flying to St Johns in the U.S. Virgin Islands we were then transported by ferry to the British Islands. Arriving in the harbour we discovered our yacht had no sails. 'Don't worry', was the response to our protestations. 'You in de Caribbean now, we don't do stress.' This was not a very constructive answer but a truthful one as after loading our bags below deck, sails were miraculously produced.

Two motley crews.

A short while later we set sail to our next port of call where we spent a very hot night. As most of the crew slept on deck it was unfortunate that almost without fail it rained at about three o'clock every morning. However, the heat dried you generally within half an hour, so getting off to sleep again was not too difficult, in fact once you got used to it the early morning shower was quite refreshing.

A visit to Richard Branson's Necker Island was limited to anchoring off shore where we were able to see or at least imagine how the other half live. Whilst there we received a radio warning of the approach of a hurricane, with urgent instructions to head for the nearest safe harbour at Road Town. As that was a day's sailing away we wasted no time in getting both yachts under way. Arriving at Road Town all the sails were taken down and stored below deck and large rubber fenders were strung round the boat as it was made fast to the jetty. Gathering all our possessions together we boarded a minibus to be moved inland to a selection of wooden huts, our accommodation while we sat out the storm.

As the weather was not too inclement we decided to go to a beach for a refreshing swim. The sea looked very strange, not much in the way of waves but what can only be described as a choppy, boiling effect. At this point we decided to make our way back to the huts arriving just as the rain came down. In minutes it was a deluge. Fortunately, our hut was on a slightly raised piece of ground unlike one of the others which soon had a river running through a bedroom and across the lounge before exiting out and into the next hut down. The wind followed but we were sheltered by the hills on three sides and on the downwind side of the island. We were pretty well confined to barracks for the next three days. Needless to say most of us were without power of any description for much of the time.

When the minibus arrived to take us back to the harbour we were glad to go, the boat had only suffered minor damage but everything below decks was wet through. The harbour master told us he had looked out of his window during the storm and saw something hovering above the harbour and grabbing his binoculars he saw it was the dinghy of a large yacht flying on its mooring rope like a child's kite about twenty feet in the air.

The other thing I remember about this holiday is that I won a competition for the 'Best Man Dressed as a Woman', but it is wise not to elaborate.

Freewheelers

The same year and we were back on dry land yet again for more adventures in my classic 1964 Jaguar Mk2 including the Irish Grand Prix Tour.

A classic car club called 'The Freewheelers' had organized a tour of Ireland principally following the route of the Gordon Bennett Race sometimes known as the Irish Grand Prix. It was created in the days when racing had been banned on public roads in Britain. The journey was fairly uneventful and we reached our first hotel just outside Dublin in good time for dinner after which we decided to sample some true Irish nightlife in a pub along the street. There was a Ceilidh band playing and everyone was having a great time, in fact one local was having such a good time that he decide to fall flat down on the floor drunk. When he couldn't be revived sufficiently to be asked to leave, the staff carried him outside and put him on the pavement where the police could deal with him without prejudicing the drinking and general enjoyment of the customers.

Part of the route included Waterford and a break to visit the Waterford Crystal Factory, but before arriving we had to find a garage for petrol. Stopping at one we pulled up at the pumps and searched around for someone to serve us and eventually a woman in the office came out rather reluctantly, and put approximately eight gallons in the Jaguar. When I asked how much it was she seemed unsure but suggested a figure that sounded about right. I paid and we continued the last few miles to Waterford parking in the Visitor Centre car park, and as is usual when we visit places of interest Irene bought a memento, in this case a crystal treble-clef ornament. There just remained a twenty mile drive to our overnight hotel stop. Starting the car and leaving the car park it seemed very sluggish and started running on about four or five of the six cylinders. It had been very hot in the car park and I wondered if it could be the result of a leaking head gasket. Straining to listen for every new rattle or different engine noise we eventually reached the hotel. I was covered by breakdown insurance so phoned the assistance number. They quickly contacted a nearby garage who arrived to check the compression on each cylinder proving to be very low on numbers three and four. I decided not have it repaired in Ireland but to let it be repatriated back home under the terms of the insurance. We were duly provided with a car which we could use for the rest of the trip but would have to leave it at the ferry port and then hire another for use back on the mainland.

Four days later the Jaguar arrived back home on a transporter and I immediately began the process of taking the engine out to be stripped down by a neighbour, who is a retired garage owner and classic car enthusiast. We had the cylinder head skimmed and new valves fitted before putting it back in the car. Confidently we started it up but it was no better. We had checked everything else and could find nothing wrong, there was now full compression on all six cylinders so what could it be? Irene then asked whether it might be the petrol that we had bought near Waterford? As it was still in the tank I drained it all out and put in two gallons of

Rix Petroleum's best. It turned over about three times on the starter motor before bursting into life running perfectly on all six cylinders. I shouted, 'You beauty!' I meant Irene not the car of course.

The adventures continued to 2001 and included a visit to the Millennium Dome in London before taking the train via the Channel Tunnel to Paris and a night at the Moulin Rouge. That trip included two memorable events, with the first occurring when we passed through the turnstiles into the Paris Metro after the show at the Moulin Rouge. Irene was slightly behind me in the turnstile to my right when a man appeared, apparently from nowhere, and grabbed her handbag. She was still in the turnstile but managed to turn around and shouted at him with such ferocity that he immediately relaxed his grip. Her shout even scared me and I hadn't done anything wrong! Realising what had happened, I turned to jump over the barrier and grab him but seeing the mixture of Irene's wrath and my impending leap he decided bizarrely to apologize before running back out of the station. Unbelievably neither of us had been aware that there had been anybody else in sight when we had entered the station.

The other event occurred at the Palace of Versailles where, when entering a room, a concealed door opened beside us and Princess Margaret emerged accompanied by uniformed officials – ignoring us completely they walked off down the corridor. A few moments later when we went outside the Princess was sitting in her chauffeur-driven Rolls Royce smoking a cigarette for a few moments before being driven away.

Later in the year we drove to Vienna to attend a concert in the State Opera House, and moving on to Saltzburg we took a trip down the salt mines that during the Second World War had been where slave labour was used to build fighter planes for the Luftwaffe. Access to the deepest part of the mines was achieved by sitting on a 45 degree sloping polished wooden pole and sliding down it at high speed all the way to the bottom!

8

My house is sold and Irene and I marry

My house 'Seasons' at Thirtleby as I have said earlier was still subject to the Agricultural Occupancy Condition, which roughly translated means it could only be lived in by someone employed in agriculture. This condition seriously limited its sale to cash purchasers only, as no building society or bank would provide a mortgage or loan on a restricted property. Consequently, my first requirement was the removal of the Occupancy Condition but to do this I had first had to prove that it was unsaleable at almost any price.

My first attempt to sell 'Seasons' and the remaining land only received an offer for the land from a neighbouring farmer, which I accepted. I then put 'Seasons' and one and a half acres on the market for £75.000 but each enquiry was stalled by the inability to obtain a mortgage. Renewed applications to the council for removal of the occupancy condition made over nearly three years continued to fail, the council giving a new reason for refusal each time, and each time we would comply with the new requirements but continue to be met with a refusal. However, with the invaluable assistance of Messrs. Dee, Atkinson and Harrison Estate Agents, their final submission was made stating the following:

'It was 1970 when 'Seasons' was built and the occupancy condition was imposed. All the surrounding houses had then been occupied by farmers or farm workers. Thirtleby comprised six farms, one market garden, one private house and four farm cottages: eleven families being employed in agriculture.

Twenty four years later in 1994 Thirtleby is comprised of three farms, eight private houses, a boarding kennels and three cottages: only four families being employed in agriculture. Consequently, if only people employed in agriculture had been permitted to move into Thirtleby during those twenty four years there would be five unoccupied houses in the village. Removing the condition will not change the nature of the village of which the property is an established part'.

This submission was accepted finally, and the council removed the Agricultural Occupancy Condition. This left me free to put 'Seasons' on the market at a realistic price and at a time to suit us.

With the weight of this obstacle off our shoulders we were at last free to set the date of our marriage; it was to be in a year's time on 29 March 2005 with both the marriage ceremony and the reception taking place at Tickton Grange, a large country house hotel near Beverley.

'Seasons' was again put on the market but this time for £295,000, it was sold in a matter of weeks for £290,000. Fifty-five years previously it had cost me £3,500 to build – maybe I should have been a builder instead of a farmer.

This prompted a mad rush to empty the house. Fortunately, a friend further down the lane had two spare garages that he kindly allowed me to use to store my goods and chattels that wouldn't be sold at the monthly furniture auction held in the Village Hall one mile down the lane in Coniston. When the removal men came to take it all down to the auction I was sitting in the last remaining chair with a cup of tea on a pile of encyclopaedias that was doubling up as a table. All they left me with was the cup of tea so I sat on the window sill. My bed had gone up to the garage store so I moved into Irene's flat while we searched round for somewhere to live.

From new builds in Bridlington to bungalows in Skidby and Cottingham we traipsed around without success. A house in Hornsea that we had looked at was sold before we could make an offer and another visit to the Skidby bungalow led to us putting in an offer, however we were told that the occupier had been delayed in moving in to his new property due to the discovery of ground contamination on its site. At this point we received a telephone call to say the Hornsea house sale had fallen through and it was now available. We made a reduced offer which was accepted and withdrew our offer on the bungalow at Skidby.

We took possession of our house in Hornsea on 4 August 2004. At this point we also had to put Irene's flat up for sale, which proved to be subject to the usual delays that seem to be the hallmark of estate agents. It is amazing how things suddenly fall in to place when you issue an ultimatum threatening to withdraw the property from the market and place it with another agent if a transaction is not completed within the week. Completion and exchange of contracts then only took a few more days. Having now sold both our properties we were able to concentrate on making the new 'Seasons' in Hornsea our home in preparation for the wedding.

The previous occupants had owned a caravan which could be parked conveniently and unobtrusively at the north side of the house behind two six foot wooden gates. We had both had previous experience of holidaying in caravans and as some of our friends were similarly equipped we decided to visit the September caravan show in Cottingham placing an order for a Sterling Eccles two berth caravan that very day; we chose this model because they were built nearby by Swift Caravans. What we didn't realise was that the salesman we had dealt with was from a dealership in Richmond more than 80 miles away. Nonetheless, aside from the distance to travel for the caravan's annual service they proved to be satisfactory suppliers.

The caravan did not arrive on the promised date but our wedding did and on the 29 March 2005 we were married. Both our families and lots of our friends attended. Our two families then totalled five daughters, four son's in-law, two grandsons and four granddaughters, and we are still counting. We both try to maintain independent responsibilities to our respective families but this does not exclude caring for all.

(left) The Bride and Groom; (right) Our families combined.

Marrying Irene has proved to be one of the best decisions I ever made. Since we first met she has encouraged in me a desire to travel or as we call it 'have adventures' and over time with a bit more persuasion I gained an interest in the classics, not just old classic cars but also music and Shakespeare.

9

Our honeymoon

The best of these adventures was in fact our honeymoon – a trip on the Eastern Orient Express from Bangkok to Singapore. We flew to Bangkok being greeted at the airport by a grey-suited young man who introduced himself as Raj requesting that we follow him to his car, a large grey Mercedes that matched his suit perfectly. He was to be our guide on behalf of the grandly named 'Holidays of Distinction', the travel company responsible for this part of our holiday. On the journey to the hotel he explained that he would be unobtrusive but was available nonetheless twenty-four hours a day giving us the telephone number on which we could contact him, as he said, 'At any time day or night'.

Arriving at the hotel the car door was opened by a uniformed gentleman whom immediately, without any apparent briefing from Raj our guide, said. 'Hello Mr and Mrs Taylor, welcome to the Mandarin Oriental Hotel.' Two girls then stepped forward and placed garlands of sweet-scented flowers around our necks. I certainly didn't get this kind of treatment at Mr and Mrs Wintle's back in Scarborough in 1946!

Our luggage was then spirited away to our rooms – yes, I did say rooms and they comprised a small sitting room, a large bedroom, and an enormous bathroom with 'his' and 'hers' of everything. The hotel's rooftop swimming pool was set twenty feet beyond a small flower-filled garden immediately below our balcony.

160

Mandarin Oriental Hotel Bangkok.

Our bedroom.

Asking us if we needed anything else this evening Raj recommended the hotel restaurant offering to book us a table on the waterside terrace where we could choose from the buffet, thus avoiding any language difficulty by being able to select only what we thought we might enjoy. We wished him goodnight asking if he would collect us in the morning at about 10.00 a.m. to show us the sights of Bangkok.

The Terrace Restaurant.

During our dinner, one of the Hotels across the Chao Phraya River had a fantastic firework display and we were actually in a better position to watch it than the guests at the hotel where it took place. The spectacle was complemented by a regular stream of dragon boats powering by and brightly lit ferry boats flitting from one bank to the other on apparently random routes swaying alarmingly as they crossed backwards and forwards through each other's wake. Occasionally one would discharge its passengers directly in front of the hotel. It was most certainly a meal to remember.

The following day, true to form, Raj was waiting in reception. He asked if I would like to have a suit made whilst we were in Bangkok, and rather fancying the idea we called in at James Fashion International where I was duly measured for a suit and quoted a price which I must say seemed a bargain. Nonetheless, I told them that in England we farmers always negotiate for a few freebies to be included, suggesting some shirts and a nice silk tie or some socks, but settling eventually for shirts for me and two silk scarves for Irene.

It was arranged that I call in for a fitting four hours later and in the meantime, we visited with Raj various temples, palaces and then to China Town amongst the stores and workshops where they make the garlands of flowers and supply floral displays for the hotels. Raj devoted the whole day to our entertainment until we went for the suit fitting at about six in the evening, for as we were scheduled to catch the Eastern Orient Express early the following morning we needed to have the suit before we departed. They assured us it would be delivered that evening and true to their word it arrived at 10.00 p.m., complete with four shirts and two silk scarves, a bargain for the equivalent of 140.00 GBP.

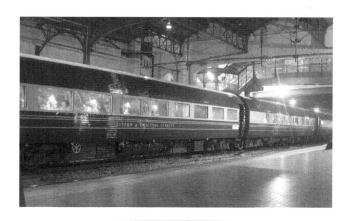

The Eastern & Oriental Express.

Raj was back on time the next morning to take us to the train. As he had been a marvellous guide spending some of his own money on more than one occasion to buy ice-cream and drinks for us all, he deserved and received a substantial tip.

On board we were shown to our en-suite cabin by our steward who provided tea and cakes while we settled in. For the first part of the journey we headed north to visit the infamous Bridge on the River Kwai.

En-suite cabin aboard the Eastern Orient Express.

Bridge on the River Kwai.

The visit to the bridge and the Kanchanaburi War Cemetery nearby was a very moving experience to which I cannot do justice by describing it here. We spent several hours touring the area while the train's engine was moved to the southern end of the carriages ready for our return south towards Kuala Lumpur and ultimately Singapore.

For dinner on our first night on board the train we had decided to dress up and do the occasion justice. Irene wore her wedding dress which had a slightly oriental look so was perfectly appropriate, and I wore my white tuxedo that I wore on my wedding day and had also been chosen with this very night in mind. We looked what might be described as a pair of 'Bobby Dazzlers'. The walk down the corridor proved a little tricky as the train was on the oldest part of the Burma railway and as a result was swaying from side-to-side bouncing us from one wall to the other, but we survived it and made our grand entrance into the dining car. Greeted by looks of astonishment from the other diners who had made no effort whatsoever to dress for the occasion, I am pleased to say that several told us later they wished they had.

Dressed appropriately.

During the meal we were entertained by the pianist and two Tai dancers who joined the train at one of the station stops along the way. The food was delicious; an incredible feat when you consider that it had been prepared in a tiny kitchen on a rocking and bumping stretch of railway line by Executive Chef Kevin Cape, a post he had held for fourteen years. We have both said many times that we have never before or since eaten such good food as he cooked for us throughout the entire journey on the Eastern Orient Express. It has never been beaten.

The Dining Car

1...   2...

3... How did Kevin do it?

With the dancers.

The following night we dressed more casually only to find our previous efforts had convinced the others to make an effort, this time leaving us as the casual ones and me looking like the Wine Waiter.

As the train continued south we passed through palm oil plantations with the occasional glimpses of the corrugated iron homesteads of plantation workers almost hidden deep in the trees. Soon the jungle began to crowd in on the track, in places almost touching the windows of our cabin as it brushed past. In our air-conditioned comfort it was hard to imagine what it must have been like for the poor prisoners working to build the railway under the cruel control of the Japanese guards. Names for sections of the line such as 'Hellfire Pass' reminded us of the suffering experienced by Australian, British, Dutch and allied Prisoners of War who were forced to work eighteen hours a day. We had been told that 69 men were beaten to death by the Japanese guards in the six weeks it took to build the cutting, and many more died from cholera, dysentery, starvation, and exhaustion. Countless other local people who had been persuaded to work on the project by offers of good wages died but were not recorded nor received a proper burial presumably not living long enough to receive any wages.

Hellfire Pass (now by-passed). Courtesy Wikipedia.
http://en.wikipedia.org/wiki/File:Hellfire_Pass_-_June_2004.jpg

Alarmingly at one of the stations the train was boarded by several Taiwan Army guards who accompanied us for the next fifty or sixty miles. They stationed themselves in the observation cars' open section at the rear, which for passengers wishing to use it for that purpose so as to experience the heavy atmosphere of the jungle, armed guards are not the most congenial company; they also might be a prime target for any terrorist with a grudge against the authorities. For this reason we either retired to our cabin or joined other like-minded travellers in the piano bar.

As the train was provisioned in Butterworth we took a day trip to Georgetown, Penang, where we were greeted by several pedal rickshaws whose drivers mostly took just one passenger at a time, with the result that by the time we had been allocated ours there was only one left, a very old and frail looking man who insisted that he could carry two people. Yet, in order to achieve this I ended up sitting half on the wheel and half on Irene's knee. Undaunted by this we set off at the rear of the convoy at an alarming speed fully aware that the first point of contact with any obstruction would be our feet which projected over the front of the seat. The extra weight had caused the driver to drop behind the rest of the rickshaw team until I made the mistake of telling him my car was a Proton made in his country. 'Oh Proton!', he shouted suddenly, finding the extra horsepower he needed to propel us faster and faster in an attempt to catch his colleagues and relay the news of his passengers' wisdom in buying a Proton.

Typical Penang rickshaw and driver. Both in better condition than ours.

Our tour from that point consisted of a series of blind corners and junctions taken at high speed with the scenery and my past life flashing before my eyes in equally rapid succession, while even my toes were curling up with the thought of acting as front bumpers on this rickety and apparently brakeless machine. He not only caught his colleagues but in his excitement sped straight through the middle of the convoy to lead the group to journey's end at the ferry that was taking us back to the mainland.

On board the train our steward had prepared afternoon tea in the cabin and it was never more welcome, the armed guards had departed and we had survived the Georgetown Rickshaw Grand Prix, a good day all told.

(left) Breakfast in our cabin; (right) Afternoon tea in the cabin.

Passing through Kuala Lumpur at about midnight our next stop was Singapore and an eagerly awaited week at the famous Raffles Hotel. On arrival at the station we were met with immaculate timing and efficiency to be guided through the formalities and driven to the Hotel, for the second time being welcomed by name by the towering frame of the six foot six inch tall Raffles Doorman.

Welcome to The Raffles.

After checking in we were taken up the polished mahogany stairs to our first floor rooms, the balcony of which overlooked the palm tree-lined white-walled courtyard. Opening the solid polished mahogany door we entered the rooms that surpassed even the luxury of those in our Bangkok Hotel.

'For Madam and for Sir': two Singapore Slings.

Sling Time.

Pausing only to drink her 'Sling' Irene made her way through a curtained archway into the large bedroom.

Bedroom.

Dressing room.

172

While Irene explored the facilities I retired to the balcony.

Our Raffles adventure would not be complete without a meal in the long bar that we duly booked and enjoyed. As up to this point and since disembarking from the train I had not had to pay for anything, so I decided to pay the dinner bill in cash and with a reasonable tip. On returning to the room it suddenly struck me that I had paid in U.S. Dollars not Singapore Dollars thus almost doubling the price in the process – now I understood the waiter's effusive thanks when I handed over the money saying I did not want any change. Being a Yorkshire man this would have ruined the whole of the remaining week and probably several months to come, so I girded up my loins and rushed breathlessly back to the Long Bar, my red face and shortage of breath giving the head waiter a clue as to my hurried return. I managed to gasp out the words 'bill' and 'U.S. Dollars', as he laid a comforting hand on my shoulder and said, 'Don't worry sir, I have not put the money through the till yet as I guessed you may have made a mistake.' Ensuring that they still received the intended tip I thanked him profusely and slunk back to our room.

After a week soaking up the sights and luxuries of Singapore, much of which can be enjoyed within the Raffles Hotel complex itself, the time came to return home with our heads full of our memories of a truly remarkable Honeymoon Adventure.

apparently his earlier rapid departure. His wife had taken, I think, a rather dim view of the damage to their car's number plate and when he saw us approaching she berated him to seek further redress. He then insisted on knowing where I would be staying for the next few weeks so I gave him a list of the campsites we intended to visit before returning to England and for good measure added our home address. As I heard no more from him I imagine he decided that buying a new number plate was the easier option.

Our journey back north through France included several days on a very dry and dusty campsite at Pont d Arc, near Vallons in the Gorges de l'Ardèche. No visit to this campsite would be complete without the wine tasting experience in the cellars of the Chateau, where you are advised to take care when finding your way back to the caravan, avoid the lake if at all possible because after all the wine, you may think you can walk on water, but trust me you can't.

Pont d'Arc.

Being from Yorkshire, we of course decided to buy the wine that we had enjoyed the most, from a supermarket in the town where we reckoned it would cost less. Pushing our trolley down the aisles we spotted the very one we had in mind piled up at the end of a row with a sign on the boxes of six bottles that said 'Offer Special 12 Euro'. A quick calculation at less than £2.00 a bottle sounded a real bargain so four boxes were piled on to our trolley.

A quick glance by the cashier at our purchases and with Eu288 flashing up on the little screen, the blood drained out of my face – the price had actually been Eu12 per bottle. Very embarrassed but like a true Yorkshireman I took three boxes off the trolleyand said we would have just the one box for Eu72 or about £65.00. When we arrived home and opened a bottle several weeks later it was so nice we thought maybe we should have bought the other three boxes.

Château de l'Epervière, Gigny-sur-Saône, Burgundy.

During the last ten days of the holiday Luxembourg, Belgium and Holland provided the last three camping sites, and our visit to Delft in Holland coincided with the days when various places were opened to the public free of charge. Irene was interested in a masonic lodge that had opened its doors for the day. We duly entered and were met by a charming gentleman who was very keen to explain the workings of his lodge. In fact he was so keen that he did not give us time to tell him we did not speak Dutch. So impressed were we by his enthusiasm that it would have been impolite to admit we hadn't a clue as to what he was saying. Fortunately our nods, 'ums' and 'ahs' must have been accepted as appropriate answers, until the very moment when we thanked him profusely in English before taking our leave.

The next day we de-camped and drove to Europort for embarkation on the Rotterdam to Hull ferry completing our 34 days and over 3000-mile European tour. Boosted by the success of the holiday we resolved to persuade some of our friends to join us the next time we ventured abroad with the caravan.

From skiers' haunts to weekend jaunts

Over the years as a founding member of the Hull White Star Ski Club we had made many friends, but from the day when I decided to put my ski boots into the skip at the rear of our Italian hotel I had only taken part in après-ski events, such as the monthly summer walks and then only to the extent of meeting everybody in the pub when they had completed the walking bit. Eventually, nine of us decided to form a group of our own that we called 'The Sideliners' on the basis that the younger generation was justifiably taking over the running of the club and we were, to put it kindly, side-lined. The 'Sideliners' meet monthly for a pub meal with the venue being chosen by each of us in turn. The 'Sideliners' comprise Ray and Julie Newmarch, Mike and Jenny Billany,

Mike and Carol Bartlett, Pat (Patricia) Lawson, and Irene and I.

In addition to our monthly get-togethers Jools (Julie) miraculously finds weekend holiday cottages for us to stay in March and November every year. As she is the youngest member of the group and by quite a few years, the passage of time has the effect of her looking more and more like a social worker organising outings for the elderly. Though to date she has not been responsible for distributing our medication, only time will tell for she is already making sure properties do not have staircases with resting places halfway up, as stopping for a breather may lead some of us to forget whether we were going up or coming down.

It is noticeable that we are getting more demanding – I prefer to call it discernible – as we get older, and en-suite becoming more important these days for the inevitable night time toilet visits.

2

New Zealand, 2007

For Irene and I any holiday lasting more than three weeks in the summer means coming back to a garden that has been at its best but then requires knocking back in to shape. Undaunted by this prospect we started to plan a month-long motorhome tour of New Zealand.

Since the days in Dad's office when he saved postage stamps from New Zealand for Geoff's stamp collection, I had harboured a desire to visit the country. The stamps were from letters sent by a seed company in Christchurch that he traded with, and when I was older he also gave me a leather wallet emblazoned with the company name, that had been sent to him in gratitude for his business over the years.

For our trip to New Zealand we were ably supported by Lisa once again at the Camping and Caravan Club's Worldwide Travel department. She booked all the flights, hotels and motorhome hire, as well as providing her invaluable advice on places to visit and things to do.

Mike and Carol agreed to join us on this particular holiday and we decided that in order to see the most of New Zealand we would hire two motorhomes. Lisa l was contacted once more and we gave her an outline of what we wanted to do. She organised our flights and hotels in Hong Kong, Christchurch, Fiji, Los Angeles and London, together with the hire of the two motorhomes in New Zealand.

Our experience at Heathrow airport was not a happy one, particularly for Carol whose luggage trolley pushed her over whilst on the down escalator and breaking her wrist. When we asked for first aid we were informed that there was no such facility in the airport and if her wrist was badly injured she would not be able to fly until she had been treated in hospital. Determined not to jeopardise the whole holiday she opted for to take the flight saying that she was fine, intending to see a doctor in Hong Kong as soon as possible on our arrival the next day.

At the doctors she was X-rayed but he only prescribed antibiotics and pain killers, surprisingly not offering to put her wrist in a plaster. Chinese medical procedures for a broken bone are obviously very different to English ones. However, Carol bought herself a support bandage which gave some relief and helped to protect it.

Hong Kong street market at midnight.

There were a few days for us in the city to enjoy the many unique experiences of the orient before flying on to Auckland on the North Island for a flight transfer to take us to Christchurch on the south island.

We spent our first night in New Zealand in a small hotel on the outskirts discovering when we awoke that England had beaten the Kiwis at Rugby back home. We tried to be muted in our celebration of this news but I am ready to admit to raising the subject in conversation more than was absolutely necessary.

Beautiful Christchurch in 2007.

Lisa had booked a complimentary first evening dinner at Le Bon Bolli restaurant in Christchurch and a most memorable meal it was. Since that time I have wondered if the restaurant had survived the catastrophic earthquake, so decided to send an e-mail enquiring its fate. Almost at the end of writing this book I received the following reply from Phillip and Helen Krail, who had been the owners in the year of our visit:

'15th October 2013

Dear John and Irene

Thank you so much for your email – and we are quite blown away that you recall your visit to Le Bon Bolli which brings back such memories. A quick update.

Le Bon Bolli was housed in a complex called Cowlishew Mews and survived the earthquakes. Unfortunately our lease expired in 2009 and with no rights of renewal left we basically had to pack up and go. Took two weeks to empty the two restaurants, private dining room, two kitchens, office etc, etc. We had to make twenty plus employees redundant (most of whom came back and helped us take the old lady apart!!). The restaurant remained empty for approximately three years until it was reopened as the Art Restaurant (which subsequently failed). After the earthquakes a well-known restaurateur (Rob Mercer) took over the lease and now operates a brassiere style bistro called 'Fiddlesticks'. The layout has changed with the restaurant only being on the ground floor – the marble staircase and art work in the dome ceiling all gone.

We went on to open a New York Style Warehouse cafe/tappas bar called the Crumpet Club (we made our own crumpets) on the corner of Tuam and Durham Street. It was a little quirky and successful. Phillip went off to work in China for a couple of years. Unfortunately the Crumpet Club building was made of bricks and concrete slabs, it survived September earthquake but came down in the February shake (Rather heart-breaking).

So – we now operate a restaurant in Sumner called Bamboozle Oriental Kitchen and Bar. (We like variety!!!).

Kindest Regards,

Helen and Phillip Krail.'

Thus, it seems you should now search out the Bamboozle Oriental Kitchen and Bar in Sumner, Christchurch.

The next day we collected our motorhomes from the depot and drove 150 miles to Omaru for one night before heading south to Dunedin, which is the second-largest city in the South Island of New Zealand, exploring the city and visiting the Albatross Colony on the Otago peninsular.

**Sheltering from 100 mph. cross-winds on the
70 mile drive to Dunedin.**

Following our stay in Dunedin we traveled 160 miles to camp at Te Aanau from which we took a day's excursion by coach and cruiser to Milford Sound, named after Milford Haven in Wales, while the Cleddau River which flows into the sound copies its name from its Welsh cousin. On our travels we mostly travelled in convoy keeping in touch with

Mike and Carol in the other motorhome by walkie-talkie radios or mobile phones and usually around mid-journey we would suggest a stop for a brew up and stretch our legs. The beauty of this way of travelling is that your kitchen comes with you and the kettle goes on at a moment's notice.

On one particular day the road seemed to be devoid of lay-bys, my body was craving the Taylor's Yorkshire Tea we had brought with us so in desperation we both pulled into a very wide farm driveway entrance leaving plenty of room to get by should the farmer come along. We were almost ready to leave when a pickup truck arrived with four dogs in the back and a 'crew cab' with the driver in the front. I quickly went over to him and apologized for occupying his driveway, his response was, 'Don't worry, I told the boss not to make it so wide if he didn't want it to be used as a parking area.' He continued, 'Are you guys in a hurry?' 'No', I said. 'Well follow me and I will take you to see the best view in New Zealand.'

Following him to park in the farm yard where we all piled into the cab of his truck as he drove up to a point 2,200 feet above the valley, from where we could see as far as Edwards Island many miles to the south and enjoy a panoramic view of all the areas where we had travelled in the past few days, as well as most of what we would be travelling through in the days to come. While we were trying to take all this in the driver was on the radio asking his wife if she could give us some lunch when we came down. We insisted we couldn't impose ourselves any further on their hospitality, though I now wish we had because they were obviously such very nice people, whom I should like to have got to know better.

As we drove down Mike told him I had been a farmer and had some sheep. 'How many?' he asked. 'Six', I replied. 'But we were mainly pig and dairy farmers on a small forty acre farm. How many do you run here?' 'The boss has 60,000 on 72,000 thousand acres', he replied. 'How many staff does that take?' I asked. 'Me and the fellows in the back', he replied pointing to the three collies and the "barker" (a dog which is trained to bark on command at any reluctant sheep during a roundup; collie sheep dogs are trained not to bark when working). He also told me that the shearing was done by a contracting gang of six men once a year.

Re-fueling at the airport.

The next most exciting adventure for Irene and I was a helicopter flight on to Mount Cook and the Franz Joseph Glacier. Mike and Carol were convinced they would never see us alive again and waited for us while drinking hot chocolate in a bar across the street. As we had been the only couple booking a flight, and two passengers only were not cost effective, we had to wait and see if anybody else turned up. Luckily one other man arrived and the pilot agreed to go with just three passengers. When all was ready we boarded and put on the headsets provided so that we could hear the pilot. Up we went at quite a rate of knots watching the town and valley falling away behind us. Soon we were over the snow fields and still climbing towards a ridge. As the helicopter crested the ridge a downdraught caused it to plunge down what seemed like several hundred feet but was probably only a few feet, exaggerated by our unpreparedness.

Our pilot was in regular contact with other helicopters in the area asking for information on safe places to land on the Glacier, and spotting some ski poles in the snow he landed gently on this fairly level marked-out area, warning us not to venture too far away because there was a danger of falling down a crevasse hidden by a covering of snow. With that discomforting thought in mind we stood a few yards in front of the aircraft, the rotors of which were turning slowly as if ready for a quick take off while our pilot left his seat to take our photograph.

Franz Joseph Glacier, Mount Cook.

On the way down he was flying all the while operating something under his seat, and reaching up he produced and handed over our photograph printed and mounted in a souvenir folder, our record of yet another adventure. Mike and Carol had by this time finished their chocolate and were very relieved to see us return in one piece and rather exhilerated by the experience.

Our journey continued along the spectacular coast road to Greymouth and thence to Kaikoura for a few days where we went whale and dolphin watching. From there we caught the Picton ferry to Wellington and the North Island section of the holiday. One of the highlights on this half of the trip took place in Rotorua, when we enjoyed a concert and Hangi (dinner) in the Tamaki Maori Village.

Chorus Line Maori Style.

The food for the three course dinner was cooked in thermal pits in the ground and after the stage show we congregated for our three course meal during which we were entertained by the master of ceremonies, who began by asking what nationalities were present and as each table in turn announced where they were from he welcomed them in their own language.

Dinner almost ready.

During the evening he spoke at least ten different languages, the whole atmosphere was one of friendship and happiness, particularly poignant when he welcomed the table next to us that comprised a party of Israelis siting with a group from Palestine. They had never met before and were all having a great time together. If only the whole world could be like this all the time. The motorhomes were returned to the depot in Auckland and we spent the next few days in the Sky Hotel, meeting a ski club friend whom several years before had moved to New Zealand and married out there.

Fiji

We enjoyed a few days in Fiji, staying in a Bure (thatched wooden hut) on a beachside complex, one that had been used by Prince Charles when making official Commonwealth visits to the island. However, his facilities were more of a bungalow than a Bure.

Our garden Bure.

The around the world flight included an unremarkable two day stopover in Los Angeles before the final leg back home.

Thankfully, we returned home on this occasion to a neatly-trimmed lawn, as we had taken the precaution of paying a local garden contractor to cut the grass every ten days or so, though this did not solve the problem of missing the best of the flowers, but as they say there is no gain without some pain.

We had some great memories to bore our chums with on the next

'Sideliners' weekend away in a large farm cottage near Staithes on the Yorkshire coast. While looking for a café on a visit to Whitby we entered one establishment and as was our usual procedure re-arranged the tables and chairs so that we could all sit together and having achieved this to our satisfaction we checked the menu that was rather disappointing. The only alternative was to leave in as orderly manner as we could until we were outside when, to use modern parlance, 'we legged it'. In our defence we have many times since re-arranged the furniture, but not before checking the menu.

Spookily one of these 'Sideliner' weekends involved a large old farmhouse at Cropton near Pickering, North Yorkshire. During breakfast the first morning of our stay Pat asked who had been using the bathroom on the third floor attic above her bedroom for she had heard footsteps during the night. Everybody denied ever being up on that floor as it wasn't a space we needed to use. The following night there were more noises followed by water leaking through the ceiling in to Mike and Jenny's room that was also situated under part of the mystery bathroom. As we were leaving the next day we simply reported the leak to the owner and forgot the incident.

Jenny recommended the farmhouse to a friend but did not mention the nightly noises for fear of putting her off. When her friend returned she told Jenny that she had enjoyed her stay except for the 'ghost' that frequented the top floor wandering in the attic during the night.

3

USA and Route 66, 2010

For many years I had been captivated by songs and stories of the famous Route 66 in America and our experience in New Zealand convinced me that organising an 'adventure' to America should be my next project.

Again who better to organize the basics of flights, start and finish hotels and hire of a motorhome than Lisa at the Camping and Caravan Club's Carefree Worldwide Holidays? A search on the internet produced details of hundreds of potential camp sites across the United States who are members of the KOA (Kampgrounds of America). Armed with this and a very good atlas of America I created a planned route which would take in a short stay in New York before heading west to pick up Route 66 somewhere near Tulsa, and then to follow it as much as is now possible to the west coast finishing with a few days in San Francisco.

If anyone would like to try this journey this was my basic route plan (opposite page).

With my 'sat nav' duly loaded with all the stopping points that would save time when travelling we set off. The few days in New York were filled with the usual round of sightseeing and a visit to the theatre to see the musical 'The Jersey Boys', the story behind the music of Frankie Valli and The Four Seasons.

Our RV (Recreation Vehicle) or motorhome was duly collected from

Route 66 USA Tour

	Miles	Drive Time	Nights	To Camp site Name & Address	Location
	200	5:00		Hilton Hotel Heathrow Airport	Car in Long Stay Car Park for Terminals 1 & 3
		H : M	1	London Heathrow Terminal 3 Virgin Atlantic Flight No VS0003 10:35am	Flight No VS0003 Depart 10:35am
Transfer to		H : M	3	"Crown Plaza, Times Square", 1605 Broadway, New York. NY 10019	Crow n Plaza Hotel Times Square. New York
Taxi to	25	1:00		Pickup RV @ El Monte. 3401 Tremley Point Road. Linden NJ 07036	El Monte Transfer from Hotel
Drive RV to	15	0:30	1	Liberty Harbor Marina & RV Park. 11 Luis Munoz Blvd' Jersey City NJ 07302	Off New Jersey Turnpike exit' Hwy 78
Drive RV to	206	4:00	2	Washington DC / Capitol KOA. 768 Cecil Avenue North, Millersville MD21108	20 miles north of Washington DC
Drive RV to	237	5:00	1	Natural Bridge / Lexington KOA. 214 Kildeer Lane. Natural Bridge. VA 24578	On Interstate 81 edge of the Appalachian Mountains
Drive RV to	270	6:00	1	Newport / Smoky Mountain KOA. 240 KOA Lane, New port. TN 37821	On Interstate 40, 10 miles east of Knoxville
Drive RV to	229	5:00	2	Nashville KOA. 2626 Music Valley Drive, Nashville. TN 37214	Nashville. near Grand Ole Opry
Drive RV to	227	5:00	2	Memphis KOA. 7037 I's-55 Marion.Marion. AR 72364	On Interstate 55. 5 miles west of Memphis
Drive RV to	171	4:00	2	Morrilton / Conway KOA. 30 Kamper Lane, Morrilton. AR 72110	I40 jctn 107 Go north on hwy 95. L at Shell Garage
Drive RV to	277	6:30	2	Oklahoma City East KOA. 6200 South Choctaw Road. Choctaw. OK 73020	Oklahoma City East
Drive RV to	300	7:00	2	Amarillo KOA. 1100 Folsom Road Amarillo TX 79108	Amarillo Texas
Drive RV to	296	7:00	2	Albuquerque Central KOA. 12400 Skyline Road NE Alberquerque NM 87123	Alburquerque New Mexico
Drive RV to	239	6:00	2	Holbrook / Petrified Forest. KOA. 102 Hermosa Drive, Holbrook. AZ 86025	From I40 exit 289, (Hwy 77. Old route 66)
Drive RV to	122	3:00	2	Grand Canyon / Williams KOA. 5333 Highway 64 Williams. AZ 86046	Interstate 40 exit 165. Hwy 64
Drive RV to	220	5:30	2	Las Vegas / Circus Circus KOA. Circus Circus Drive, Las Vegas. NV 89109	Las Vegas
Drive RV to	153	3:30	1	Barstow / Calico KOA. 35250 Outer Highw ay 15 north, Yermo CA 92398	On highw ay 15. Barstow
Drive RV to	207	4:30	1	Visalia / Fresno Sth. KOA 7480 Ave 308, Visalia. CA 93291	From Hwy 99 take Hwy 198 East to Plaza dr. exit
Drive RV to	130	3:00	1	Yosemite West / Mariposa KOA 6323 Hwy 140, Mdpines CA 95345	On Scenic Hwy ay 140. 23 mile west of Yosemite
Drive RV to	143	3:00	1	Brannan Island KOA. 922 West Brannan Island Road, Isleton CA 95641	From Interstate 5, take Hwy 12 (Lodi Exit)
Drive RV to	60	2:00		RV Drop off @ El Monte RV. 6301 Scarlett Court, Dublin. CA 94568	Off Hwy 101.
Transfer to	45	1:00	3	Comfort By The Bay Hotel. 2775 Van Ness Ave. , San Francisco, CA, US, 94109	El Monte Transfer to Hotel
Transfer to	19	0:30		Airport Flight home Virgin Atlantic Flight No VS0020 Depart 16:55am	Arrive Heathrow 4th July 11:05am
Arrive Home	3591	83.00	32	Total nights	
			26	Hire days / nights	

Coast to Coast USA, Route Plan.

the depot in New Jersey and following the usual trip to a supermarket we joined the rush hour traffic on the New Jersey Turnpike, five lanes each way bumper to bumper. Although the sat nav was telling me to turn right across five lanes of oncoming traffic my brain was saying 'no way', until I saw in the distance a traffic light that every now and then stopped all the oncoming lanes in their tracks. Edging over into the right lane I got the green light and survived the crossing. A few miles further we reached our camp site for the night, not a very inspiring one but welcome nonetheless.

Waiting for the morning rush hour to subside the next day we hit the trail or more precisely drove down the Turnpike once more, without incident we thought. Much later we discovered that we had missed a toll booth and had become road traffic offenders on the run!

Washington was interesting but we were itching to see the countryside and were amply rewarded by the journey to the KOA's campsite, Natural Bridge Lexington. That evening, and once settled on the site, we were entertained by the sight of hundreds of fire flies, their little pin pricks of light zooming about amongst the trees in Nature's partnership dance.

The scenery as we drove west through the Appalachians and along the Smoky Mountain highway, was green, clean, and fresh. A one night stop in Newport preceded our 270 mile leg to Nashville, with our drives accompanied by the appropriate country music on the radio or CD player in the RV. As we arrived at the Nashville KOA we discovered that a few days previously they had had 12 inches of rain in 48 hours flooding most of the town and the camp site.

Their first response to our request for a pitch was, 'Sorry, we have nowhere dry for you to park, we are full.' My hangdog look, in addition to informing them that we had travelled all the way from England, persuaded them to find us a suitable pitch. This required an enormous forklift tractor to bodily pick up a log cabin-type bungalow that had been washed of its foundations by the flood and move it elsewhere on the site.

The good news for us was that we had arrived in the middle of Country Music Festival week when there are the favourite and famous bands and singers of the country music scene performing everywhere in the town, from parking lots to street corners and car showrooms, in fact anywhere with a space big enough to have an impromptu show. Legends Corner Bar was one example where the resident band invited an 11-year old youngster on to the stage when he had asked if he could join them. He wanted to play the drums and they looked somewhat sceptical as he climbed on stage but when he started to play they joined in and people stopped drinking and applauded, hooted, and whistled their appreciation.

It had been an ambition of mine to go to a show at the original 'Grand Ole Opry' theatre which had been moved recently to a new purpose-built theatre in the town. However, because the new venue had been flooded the show had returned to its historic home, The Rymans Theatre, and it was possible, if we stayed in Nashville one more night than the schedule

Legends Corner Bar, Nashville.

allowed, we could get tickets. It was too good an opportunity to miss even at the cost of two 350 mile drives to make up lost time in the next two days.

**Dolly Parton at the Grand Ole Oprey' theatre,
Nashville Country Music Festival, 23 April 2005.**

Oklahoma City justified two nights stay giving time to explore its history, accurately depicted by a group of bronze statues commemorating the Land Run of 1889. On 22 April of that year, the unassigned lands were opened up to 50,000 Americans, when thousands of competitors on wagons, horses, or on foot, rushed to stake out their claims, each vying for 160 acres, known as a 'town lot'. However, some unscrupulous people crept out the previous night and hid in the undergrowth to be ready to emerge and grab the best land.

Our first taste of Route 66 came just south and less than '24 hours from Tulsa' as the song goes. Route 66 is also known as the Will Rogers Highway or Main Road America, and for us this is the where we began, in the words of the song, to 'Get our kicks on Route 66'. We switched

Land Run of 1889.

on the cruise control and the CD player and sang along to all the tunes we associated with the West and Route 66.

Seligman, the town where the re-marketing
of 'Historic Route 66' began.

No need to go hungry on Route 66.

A couple of days later and a few hundred miles further west into Texas, the CD was playing 'Is This the way to Amarillo?' and would you have it, it was! And there we camped. Home of The Big Texan restaurant best known for its 72 ounce (4.5 pounds/2.04 kg) steak, nicknamed 'The Texas King'. The steak is free to anyone who, in one hour or less, can eat the entire meal, consisting of the steak itself, bread roll with butter, baked potato, ranch beans, shrimp cocktail, and salad, otherwise, the meal costs $72.00. Those who have successfully consumed the Texas King meal have their names recorded and posted at the restaurant. As of 15 March 2011, over 8,800 people out of approximately 50,000 have accomplished this feat. The record for the shortest time needed to finish the entire Texas King meal is held by competitive eating champion Joey Chestnut. He finished the challenge in 8 minutes and 52 seconds. Should I try it? I would rather take my time and pay for it.

Moving on and passing through the Painted Desert and Petrified

Forest we made our way to Williams and the Grand Canyon. Checking in to the Williams KOA the receptionist insisted I should say the word aluminium, which I duly did. She responded by calling her friends' mates so they too could hear the Brit saying 'aloominium'. Once again I obliged and satisfied that the British 'do speak funny' everyone went back to work.

Our next stop was to be in Las Vegas, every bit as brash as we expected, a bit like Blackpool on steroids. We took in all of the recommended sites discovering that once inside a casino it is almost impossible to find the exit. We had opted to take a short cut from our campsite at the rear of Circus Circus Hotel through its Casino to the Strip, eventually having to retrace our steps to get out. We decided in future that we would go the long way round!

A few days later in Yosemite National Park, rapidly failing brakes

Staring into the abyss from the South Rim of the Grand Canyon.

forced me to drive the last 100 miles using the handbrake and then only when absolutely necessary, ending the journey to the RV depot near San Francisco without even the benefit of the handbrake. Safely parked, I negotiated a 50 dollar discount, only to have this completely wiped out by the news that I was 'wanted' by the New Jersey Highway Patrol for a traffic violation for I had missed, as already mentioned, the pay booth on the New Jersey Turnpike, requiring payment of a fifty dollar fine else I would not be permitted to leave the country. I blame the sat nav.

Four days of relaxation and seeing the sights in San Francisco ended our 4,000 mile drive coast-to-coast across the USA and Route 66.

Back to Yorkshire

In between our adventures abroad the pull of Middlesmoor continues and over the past few years we have returned for the Nidderdale Agricultural Society Show in September held in Bewerley Park Pateley Bridge and on one occasion took our caravan and those of friends Ray and Julie to the Walker family's Studfold Caravan Park at Lofthouse, just two fields away from Hazel Close and How Stean Gorge. Another event which drew us back as it does each year for many people with memories of life at Middlesmoor is The Bell Festival, which is held on or around 11 June. It dates from 1868 when a peal of six bells was given by Mary Ann Barkwith to the church in memory of her uncle Simon Horner, a local man and Hull merchant, the founder of Middlesmoor School.

The procession is led from the centre of the village down to the Church by the Lofthouse and Middlesmoor Silver Band for a service in the church and a children's tea in the old school building, now the village hall, and a fete which when we last visited in 2007 was held in

The Bell Festival procession in Middlesmoor.

what had been the school playground and adjacent field used for the school sports days back in the 1940s.

So no matter how far we roam we still return to our familiar and beloved territory of Yorkshire.

Postscript: or leaning on the farm gate

On reaching this stage of my memoir, I decided to take a relaxed look at what had changed in the world of farming since I retired, so for a start I went to the newsagents and bought the latest edition of *Farmers Weekly*.

I was horrified by the amount of form-filling that farmers have to do now, most of it to comply with EEC rules and regulations, a chore which our so-called European partners generally ignore and more importantly get away with ignoring.

Cows that used to have names like Topper and a herd prefix like Taybro, required nothing more than a pencilled-in standard outline drawing, and only then if they were pedigree animals, whereas all cattle are required these days to have their own 'Passport' which travels with them everywhere.

If your children want to take their pet piglet for a walk in the lane you now need a licence for pig walking and would probably have to kill it before you could bring it back home. Just imagine the crying children if this was to happen!

I will never understand why there can be millions of people starving in the world whilst we farmers have been paid to leave fields devoid of crops and not even allowed to plough and cultivate them as a fallow break for fear of improving the following year's yield. I cannot understand it but I do know why it has happened; it was to protect the incomes of inefficient farmers in other European countries from more efficient British farmers who are able to produce more and thereby cheaper grain.

But it's better that I do not get started on the EEC and return to looking over the gate at what's happening in the field.

We used to take pride by ploughing in perfectly straight lines, not any more. Now you start at any field edge, straight or like a dog's hind leg, and with a reversible plough with which you can go back and forth across the field until you reach the other side. You simply do what we used to call rather disparagingly 'black it over'. In fact more and more farmers are not ploughing at all, simply cultivating a seed bed with power harrows and tractors with their fuel tanks filled with gallons of expensive diesel – sorry, that should now be litres of diesel. For proper ploughing I would need to go to a ploughing match.

Straight just like it should or used to be done.

However, I do like the use of technology when it allows farmers to apply chemicals and fertilisers more precisely, treating almost every square metre individually, and by being located by satellite permitting application rates to be controlled by a computer using data based on soil tests and yield information gathered by the combine when harvesting the previous crop. Information, which in the old days, would not be available until the stack of sheaves had been thrashed during the winter or spring, and then only on an estimated yield per field not metre by metre as is now possible.

Livestock farming has similarly evolved with the emphasis on welfare and quality of the end product. A typical example of the modern farmer is Peter Kirkwood who was the first farmer to sell his pigs on my Tabrotec Computerised Auction and continued to do so until I closed it down. He now grows the grain on his farm which is fed to his pigs, some of which are then sold direct to a leading supermarket, with the remainder providing the pork product for his farm shop, along with the locally produced lamb and beef that he sells to his customers.

If Tabrotec did nothing else I hope it played some part in showing farmers that they do not have to go to livestock markets and take whatever they are given on the day. Livestock do not have to be transported all over the country, and consumers don't have to pay extra for the middle men who make a good living by nodding their heads at an auction. I never met one who had gone home broke. Farmers now know that by doing their own marketing they can receive a fair return for quality meat products which in turn benefits the animals that have been so carefully nurtured, and most importantly the consumer who is able to buy wholesome nutritious food which has been produced with great care using the best practices of animal welfare.

Finally

I have concluded that who we are is a mixture of our history, over which we had no control, our upbringing over which our parents had much control, and the successes and failures over which we have some control.

I believe this may have given me an experience of life which dares me to offer some guidance to those much younger, though I will try to remember that tomorrow's world will be their world and the choices and decisions are ultimately for them to make. My forebears created a world which gave me the opportunity to make mistakes and achieve some success in roughly equal measure. Those who come after me, will, no doubt as I have done, experience both pain and pleasure along the way.

There is an old farming saying which is well worth remembering:

Live as if you were going to die tomorrow.
Farm as if you were going to live forever.

This brings me full circle, for now I am basking in the love I have for my ever-growing family, who have given me so much happiness over what has now become 76 years of which it could be said: 'Tha should 'ave seed it coming lad.' Only by reading this book seventy years ago could I have done that.

Glossary

A.I. man Artificial Insemination Service operative.

Allowance The mid-morning or mid-afternoon refreshment for farm workers in the field.

Barley Awn Brittle whisker like appendage of barley can appear in other corn crops.

Barrage Balloons A large Balloon tethered with a steel cable to deter low flying enemy aircraft.

Brawn A traditional classic dish of the meat from a pig's head and trotters cooked in a vegetable and spice stock that is then used to form a jelly that sets around the meat.

Bushel Scuttle Tub-like container for measuring corn by volume.

Chaff Corn Husks and chopped up pieces of straw, sometimes referred to as Kaf.

Digs A boarding house.

Grouse Beating Walking across the moor to drive the grouse up into the air and towards the guns.

Hay Sledge Large wooden platform on steel shod runners for transporting hay cocks.

Hay Sweep A six foot wide wooden frame with long forward pointing wooden tines dragged by a horse to gather rows of hay into heaps.

Heifer Cow before it has had a calf.

Luck Money Handing back part of the payment for livestock as thanks or in place of a guarantee.

Midden Dump for domestic waste of all kinds.

Shrapnel Splintered pieces of bombs or shells.

Tow'd Yorkshire dialect meaning 'The Old'.

Tumbled and Kiss't Floor Fell face down on to the floor.

Further reading

Jennings, Bernard, and Pateley Bridge Tutorial Class, *A History of Nidderdale*, (The Advertiser Press Ltd), 1967.

Lee, Dinah, *Middlesmoor. A Stones-Throw From Heaven*, (Avenue Printing House), 2004.

Olsenn, W., and Russell A., *The Complete Route 66 Lost and Found*, (Voyageur Press), 2008.

Shernoff, Howard, and Samofalova, Tanya, *Russia by River*, (Rikki-Tikki-Tavi, Inc.), 1996

Upper Nidderdale Local History Group, *People and Places*, (Upper Nidderdale Local History Group), 2008.

Walton, Samuel King, *Pig In A Poke. The Ramblings of a Country Peasant*, (Clio Publishing), 2007.

Clio Publishing is a small independent company with a growing reputation for providing bespoke publishing answers for authors and researchers in the humanities, arts and social sciences. The speed, flexibility and cost-efficiency of print on demand digital technology combined with the marketing opportunities of the internet, direct mail, social networking, and 4G mobile communications now offer authors powerful new ways of exploiting their intellectual property and creative ideas.

If you are an author in the arts, humanities, and social sciences, that would like to take charge of your publishing destiny, then why not email the publisher, Dr Susan England at clioclio@outlook.com

http://www.cliopublishing.org